discover your
inner
sloth

discover your inner sloth

mix in its leisurely dynamic to banish stress
before it ruins your life and relationships

gillian bridge

foulsham

LONDON • NEW YORK • TORONTO • SYDNEY

foulsham

The Publishing House, Bennetts Close, Cippenham,
Slough, Berkshire, SL1 5AP, England

Foulsham books can be found in all good bookshops and direct from
www.foulsham.com

ISBN-13: 978-0-572-03287-6
ISBN-10: 0-572-03287-0

Copyright © 2007 Gillian Bridge

Cover illustration © Jack Pittman

A CIP record for this book is available from the British Library

Printed in Great Britain by Creative Print and Design (Wales), Ebbw Vale

Contents

Going nowhere fast

Life is too precious simply to let it slip away. Can there be anyone out there who doesn't believe that? Yet how many people today find themselves wondering whatever happened to an hour, a day, or even the greater part of a week? You know that slightly alarming feeling that follows the question,

Was it this week or last that I drove into London?

Is it just my imagination or are more people – of all ages, and not merely the moribund – experiencing that sensation more of the time?

And what about being utterly convinced that you are working hard to lead the fullest of lives, yet not being quite certain you are succeeding because some of the best parts seem to have gone walkabout in an alien time zone?

Oh God, yes! Of course I remember!

But of course you hadn't remembered, not at first, had you? You'd had to scrabble in some strange, dark and silent place to retrieve the missing bits of your history.

So many demands are being made on our time and attention. They creep up on us, silently but relentlessly, like armies of robotic ants.

What should I do first?
How can I prioritise?
What must I remember?

At the end of another grindingly long day, do you ever feel that everything might be fine if only you could somehow catch up with yourself, instead of trailing along behind like the back end of a bendy bus?

You are not alone if you feel that great chunks of your time on this earth seem to be vanishing into a giant black vortex. More and more of us are living life in such a spin of speed and fury that if we were to stop for five minutes, we'd probably crash dizzily to the ground.

But let us take the risk and stop for that five minutes. That brief pause might give us time to reflect on just what we are getting out of this great whirl of activity, this life of go, go, go. What is it all about when, in this crazy, topsy-turvy world of ours, even a leisure centre is a place of sweat and toil?

So let's stop, give ourselves five minutes to catch up and, as the song says, 'think it over'.

MEMORIES – THE RESERVOIRS OF OUR LIVES

Just imagine for a moment that you had been kidnapped and thrown into a cave with no company but your memories; just how good would your company be? Okay, so it's an unlikely idea, but the question is a serious one, because memories are like the reservoirs of our lives. If we don't have a decent supply of memories, how can we ever be sure that our lives are as full as we boast?

And full should not be confused with busy, because a life that is merely busy will only provide us with such comforting memories as the irritating, traffic-laden, journeys we take to work each morning; the arguments we have with our sat-nav; the snatched sandwich lunches we eat before interminable meetings over key performance targets; the school runs we go on which morph seamlessly into after-school activities; the trips we 'enjoy' to Ikea and Tesco; and the ever longer hangovers we suffer after nights spent 'having a good time'. No, busy is not at all the same thing as full; we'd find our time in the cave might be spent much more pleasantly in the company of less stressful memories than those.

Wouldn't it be better to have memories to focus on such as summer picnics with the children, moonlight strolls, daft games with our pets, fun times with lovers, the smell of early morning in spring, holding a new baby in our arms, laughter with friends? Memories of times when the moment finally gets to take over from the movement.

If, like me, you're beginning to feel that while busyness and movement have their place, you'd quite like to have enough memories to keep you amused until the SAS turn up, then it's time you started to redress the balance and concentrate rather more on those significant *moments* in your life.

SIGNIFICANT MOMENTS

When I set out to do some research into the things that people really did find significant – those moments they remembered and prioritised when they had to take five at some point in their lives – I found kidnap victims to be in rather short supply. Luckily, I was working with prisoners at the time (who are also quite practised at taking five), so I asked groups of them for their thoughts on the subject instead. No matter what their individual differences in terms of circumstance, sentence length or culture of origin, when they were asked what was really important to them while they were inside, their answers were almost always the same.

They didn't dwell particularly on memories of big houses, nice wheels, fine clothes or good food. None of them reminisced fondly over DIY, texting, internet browsing or going shopping; in fact, not a single one of our supposedly favourite activities rated a mention, and for some of the prisoners the very thought of returning to those aspects of the rat race was actively unpleasant. What really mattered to them and kept them going, they said, were the following memories:

- My kids, my kids, my kids, my kids (this was said more than anything else) – in particular, the smell of my kids, the touch of my kids, the sound of my kids.
- My wife, girlfriend or partner (usually only one at a time).
- Sex (usually accompanied by, 'Sorry about this one'!).
- Fishing.
- Walking the dog, especially in the spring.
- Being able to go for a long walk on my own.
- Having a quiet night in/out, with my mates/girlfriend.
- Running through the fields.
- Having a meal with my family.
- Being told off by my mum.
- Sitting on the settee, surrounded by my family.

- Having a good old row with my missus.
- Going down a street where people know me.
- Seeing someone smile at me and mean it.

None of these sounds too complicated or demanding, does it? We all, whatever our circumstances, prefer to prioritise and remember warm, tactile, life-enhancing, simple moments.

So why is it that when we have them ready to hand we never seem to rate such things highly enough? What makes us keep on pushing forward and rushing to 'make progress' or 'have a good time' when so often we already have what really should be the ultimate goal, sitting on the sidelines of our lives, patiently waiting for us to slow down enough to appreciate it?

So if we want to have more quality experience in our lives – the kind of experience that's going to be worth remembering, that will make us feel our lives are fuller and enhanced in all kinds of ways – how can we achieve this?

MEETING UP WITH THE SLOTH

This is not an academic treatise, so we're not going to paddle deeply in the intellectual mire and trample on the toes of psychologists, anthropologists, sociologists or policy-makers – well, not purposefully anyway. What we are going to do is take a perhaps rather jaundiced look at some of the madder aspects of the way we live now, considering whether there is actually anything of real value in them for us. We are then going to encounter one of the oldest creatures around, one that has lived happily within its environment for thousands of years without managing to destroy very much of it, and see if it has anything to teach us about pacing ourselves for more rewarding living.

This book is intended as a celebration of the sloth and an exploration of what the sloth's habits can offer us – which it will get around to showing us all in its own good time. (You may be surprised to learn that – despite the sloth's reputation – it isn't all about laziness.) By the time you reach the end of the book, you are going to feel that it's okay to get pleasure from the things that, deep down, most of us already seem to think matter far more than the apparent priorities in the frantic lives we're leading at the moment.

RUNNING AHEAD OF OURSELVES?

Of course, some of the problems this book will be looking at are far from unique to our twenty-first-century lifestyle. People have always grumbled that there is too much to do, and whole generations and cultures have suffered from being overworked in infinitely worse ways than we are today. However, there is perhaps something particularly perverse, or perhaps particularly poignant, about today's problems, because at one stage in very recent history we were apparently offered an option. Anyone born before 1960 will know that the post-war, largely post-Industrial Revolution, generation saw leisure as the way forward. Newspapers and glossy magazines of the time were full of images of laid-back people drifting through calm and uncluttered landscapes. In the 1950s and 60s, the way all this was going to be achieved was through the development of technology. Technology was going to take the hard grind out of work, and life was going to be what was left: a leisure-driven breeze. And so we embraced technology, and by doing so we *chose* the frenzied lifestyles we now follow.

Unfortunately, technology has turned out not always to be so user-friendly after all, and the benefits of a number of decades of technological development have been sketchy, to say the least. It's true that our households are now much easier to run, and the opportunities for communication are vastly expanded. But what about our workplaces, many of which have been completely revolutionised by the advent of the computer? It seems here that for every task made simpler by technology, another one has been added to the list of things to do. According to recent research, 82 per cent of office workers in 1994 felt that, in an average week, they had completed half their daily tasks; the proportion of office workers who feel they can say the same today is only 50 per cent. Apparently, all that computerised systems, e-mails, scanners, mobiles, texts, the internet, the intranet and so on have done for us is to make us feel that there is even more that we could, or should, have been able to do each day. What happened to making life easier? Where did leisure get lost in all of this?

Sometimes it looks as though it died in the embrace of technology. Is there a beach, a funfair, an event of any kind that isn't littered with people busily dividing their leisure experience into pixels? The advent of digital cameras and camera-phones has meant that life is now seen through a lens and then remembered on a screen: reel memories, not real memories. These are not easily found in our heads.

Perhaps that is because our heads are too full already – with all the information that bombards us daily from all that technology. Apparently, it's having much the same effect on our heads as it is on our working day. There's so much to deal with, we think we are never finished. We have attention overload, and that means we end up unable to distinguish the significant from the trivial. We have no time to process the important things – which leaves us feeling cross and frustrated. And because this is the twenty-first century, this phenomenon has to be defined as a syndrome – Attention Deficit Trait – and a lot of us are suffering from it.

Perhaps regretfully, perhaps gleefully – depending on how sloth-like our natural tendencies are – we may have to conclude that we are only ever going to be able to do, or even think, a finite amount of stuff, no matter how much technological support (or interference) we have around us. If that's true, taking on more and more tasks, and more and more information, can only ultimately lead to failure on a larger and larger scale.

But most of us don't set out to fail – quite the reverse – so is it simply human arrogance that prevents us from accepting that we may only be capable of finite achievement, or is there a little more to it than that? Could it even be that this tendency of ours to assume we need to keep doing more is part of our pre-programming for survival? After all, if what we really, really want (or think we really, really want – when we have the opportunity to take time out to think) is as simple as the prisoners on page 9 said, why do we so rarely feel satisfied with our achievements, and why, when we have technological slaves, do we feel we should be doing more and more ourselves?

THE FLIPSIDE OF DARWIN

It's possible that the answers to these questions lie in our evolutionary past, when taking time out may have equated with death by inattention, and survival of the fittest meant getting one over on your neighbour. Maybe we are genetically programmed to reject ease because it puts us at risk of being eaten by something large and unpleasant. Perhaps we are hardwired to struggle and fight in order to get to the top and enjoy the best view.

After all, half the human population of the planet today still have to struggle minute by minute to survive; and even in comfortable, modern Western societies, the good life has only arrived for the majority of us in the last few decades – within the last few seconds to midnight on the evolutionary clock. It's not that long since most water was collected from a common pump, not that long since large families 'hot-bedded', and not that long since the majority of people thought travel meant going to the local market town and that holidays were religious festivals. It's also only 60 years since half the major cities in Europe lay in ruins. If we are not basking in our relatively blessed state today, and if we don't want to believe we are irredeemably cynical, there must be a reason, mustn't there? We must have some deep-seated need to make things difficult for ourselves, to up the ante.

Why else would we still be trying to make life faster and faster, and fuller and fuller? Why would a species naturally want to be on the go 24/7? And why would we have glamorised frenzy and made speed iconic? Why aren't we more conscious of the absurdity of rushing to a yoga class or driving to a recycling facility?

We find ourselves living in a ramped-up world of constant speed, furious energy, hyperactive involvement in anything and everything, and endless stimulation and consumption. Not only do we expend energy and money on recycling things that were mostly unnecessary in the first place – apparently so that we can stimulate our sense of self-worth by telling ourselves that we're saving the planet – but we also fill our heads with unnecessary and stress-inducing information at every turn, often at the insistence of governments that simultaneously tell us they are interested in our health and welfare! No wonder many of us are so confused that we end up spending a fortune on counselling and blood pressure pills, partly to treat the stress created by worrying about the fortune we've spent.

THE 'C' WORDS: CHOICE AND COMMITMENT

Choice, the mantra of successive governments, whose virtue is practically a given not only in politics but also in therapy sessions, is one of the most controversial outcomes of our drive for expansion. Every manufacturer claims to want to give it to us, and every consumer champion demands our right to it, but does more choice actually give us what we want, or even what we think we want? Or does it, in fact, lead to yet more overload – followed by yet more confusion?

For example, the seemingly endless choices now available to 20- and 30-somethings means that they are actually making fewer and fewer fundamental decisions about what to do with their lives. The glossies and the Sundays now regularly refer to a new social group they call Yeppies, short for Young Experimenting Perfection-seekers, and these people just don't do commitment. If you believe the magazine articles, half the inhabitants of London, New York, Sydney and just about all the big cities of the Western world are simultaneously shopping for perfect lifestyles in the great department store that is urban life, and are only stopping shopping for long enough to rest their weary feet in the coffee lounges that are their parents' suburban homes. It's not that Yeppies are lazy, though: *Young Ones*-style hippy indifference is not at all their thing. Yeppies probably care too much – about what they should be doing, where they should be going, who they should be settling down with, how they should be looking, what foods they should be eating, what drinks they should be drinking, and so on ... and on.

Whether or not Yeppies really exist – and, as in so many other areas of our life, we should check that against reality as we know it (more on that later) – there is undoubtedly an exhausting series of options made available to young people today. You can spend the morning dressed as an entrepreneur, slip into conservation guise for the afternoon, and then experiment with designer stardom in the evening. The prospects, the wardrobes and the potential for riches seem to be endless – provided you don't confine potential with commitment.

THE DEBT PRESSURE

In the meantime, of course, while we are all so busy deciding what we want to be and do when we grow up, there are costs. But, hey, you can save yourself a fortune, bung it on the plastic, nought per cent finance! Even people old enough to know better fall for this one. In a *Sunday Times* article in 2005 a, no doubt extremely well paid, journalist bemoaned the debt she and her family had got themselves into, which included a mere £40,000 on credit cards. How many take-aways, flat-screen TVs, designer suits and holidays in Tuscany can a family *need*? If even a middle-aged, well-paid, intelligent person is seduced by choice to the tune of £40,000, no longer knowing how to limit their aspirations and pretensions, how on earth can we expect the generation one down from there to cope? In pretty much the same way, seems to be the answer to that question, since ever greater numbers of young people appear to be building up mountainous levels of debt, but without the same level of income as older people or the cash pot of a relatively cheaply bought property to cushion the impact of any calling-in of debts.

All of which puts younger people under even more pressure, and it's a pressure that seems to be kicking in earlier and earlier. Students, whose duty for generations has been to lead lives of unfettered debauchery so they can get it out of their system before going on to lead blameless lives as accountants, are now so saddled with debt they are in depression freefall. British universities spend a total of £30 million a year on counselling services for students coming to terms with the need to earn enough money to pay for their course, keep up their required alcohol intake and pay the mortgage on their friends' parents' pension plan houses (single rooms only, please – which self-respecting student today would share?).

And never mind people of student age, apparently we now also have consumption-induced depression in children as young as five. Which at least is a variation on the consumption-induced depression of a hundred years ago!

THE DREAM

It seems that what may well be a Darwinian urge to stay ahead of the game, coupled with an avalanche of choice that just was not available to earlier generations, has brought us to where we are today. And yet, if our prisoners are to be believed (and why not?), where we are is not necessarily where we would be in our dreams. In our dreams, apparently, we want to be with our families, idling some, at least, of our time away, chewing the fat with our mates, and, if not exactly dancing through the daisies, then strolling around the countryside on a summer's day and watching the dog do most of the work.

THE REALITY

It seems that we are suffering from a surfeit of everything: from interventions and activity to information, technology and choice, all of which leaves us too busy to enjoy any of it properly. Overall, that doesn't appear to be making us very happy or relaxed.

Excess is everywhere, not just in our consumption of goods. We spend too much of our lives sitting on tarmac, for example. Typically, an urban professional might spend 24 hours out of a 14-day period making their way from A to B, not going anywhere special, just getting to work.

And then there's the visual overload on that tarmac. Perhaps it's time we asked for our scenery back. Research suggests that the proliferation of white signs, red signs, blue signs, yellow boxes, yellow lines, white lines, red concrete, grey concrete, traffic lights, flashing lights is a self-defeating strategy. The more we have, the less we see. In experiments in Wiltshire, England, when most of the signage and lineage was removed, and in Barnet, also England, when road humps were removed, the number of road accidents actually went down – but still planners are putting more signage, lineage and humps in.

It's not just visual inflation that's creeping in, there's auditory inflation, too. Once upon a time, when a lorry backed down the road, people had to nip out of its way. Then a warning sound was added, then a voice helpfully telling us the lorry was on the move. Now it seems that even the voice is insufficient to get the message across because with each increase in auditory intervention, there has been less response. Result: to get the same outcome as before, more and more has to be done. So the noise a lorry makes as it backs is being made louder.

Then there's divorce, which is at an all-time high. At first sight that suggests that fewer of us actually do want to spend time with the person we once saw as 'the one'. But a recent report suggested that as one-third of the UK working population works longer than an eight-hour day, some couples barely get to spend *any* time together, let alone quality time. A quarter of the couples surveyed only see their partners at home twice in a week. 'Working late at the office' is no longer just an excuse. In 1946, 54 per cent of women cited infidelity and violence in divorce suits, against 8 per cent of women citing husbands' long working hours. The second figure has now grown to 28 per cent. (There's no mention of what men might cite.)

These are just a few random examples of the reality of the all-round escalation of everything, the excess that we take for granted in our daily lives. Our daily lives filled with so much that is not exactly conducive to ease or relaxation, it's hardly surprising if the modern world is rather less wonderful than the gentler version we dream about.

MARKERS OF A JITTERY SOCIETY

It's not only impoverished students that are going to their doctors with depression; according to national statistics, 10 per cent of the British population are suffering from depression at any given time – that's approximately 6,000,000 people in Britain today. And depression is not specific to people who don't have enough of what our consumer society offers, it hits high-achievers too. Only recently, a successful lawyer jumped to her death from a tall building, apparently because she was suffering from clinical depression. Perhaps the cause of her depression was pressure at work, because apparently 500,000 Britons are suffering from work-related stress at any time, too.

In a recent survey, more than 65 per cent of people questioned said they had trouble sleeping, and one in three of them said they had less than five hours' sleep a night (the rest of the night presumably being spent worrying about credit card debt and wondering whether they've made the right choice of carpet or lifestyle).

Rates of addiction, which is the most natural of all outcomes of excess, because it mirrors it, are growing all the time. Drink, drugs, gambling, texting, keeping fit, relationships, love, there's virtually nothing we don't do to excess these days – but excess in these things doesn't make us happy. Addiction is hell for most addicts, and for all those around them, and thousands of people seek treatment every day.

Shopping has become one of the most common addictions of our time. In the past, people enjoyed some precious time out during religious festivals, but not any more. A typical Christmas or Easter sees thousands of us desperately trying to find a shop that's open (not that difficult in most towns). Anything we can buy, we will buy, no matter how horrible it is or how many other similar things we have that would probably do. Why else would anyone buy some of the things to be found in pound shops – or in Harrods, for that matter?

Then there's food to go. Clearly, Henry Mayhew, a social commentator in the nineteenth century, didn't foresee this becoming one of the emblems of a thriving new world. Criticising the conditions of London's poor, he said that people having to eat their food on the streets was one of the most significant indicators of deprivation. It wasn't only, he said, that it showed they had no time to sit and eat, but also that it demonstrated their failure to understand the principles of good nourishment.

Which leads on to manners, which seem to have been replaced today by personal need. Forget the pleasant social interactions of our neighbourhood street – dreamed of by one young prisoner. Manners take time, as in waiting patiently in queues, giving up our place to somebody whose need is greater than our own, making that wrong turn rather than holding up all the traffic while we selfishly correct our move, letting a car out of a side street, not shoving our way onto a crowded bus, allowing ourselves to be politely bored by the company of

someone who isn't *exactly* to our taste, sending thank you letters. And also as in, *not* eating greedily in the street.

OVER-ENGINEERED FOR TODAY?

All of these things, these markers of a jittery society, are the result of too many of us feeling driven, pressured and time-limited – which is absurd really, because it means we have no advantage over Stone Age people, who relied on hunting their food to survive and spent most of their short lives anxious, agitated and on the go. Times may have moved on, but perhaps our survival strategies haven't.

Our survival drive may now actually be destroying the pleasure we should be getting from lives that are the fulfilment of our parents' and grandparents' dreams and ambitions. We have what they wanted: security, peace, time and leisure. But we are busily (*very* busily) throwing a lot of it away.

SLOTHLY DOES IT

This is where the inner sloth can help us.

Sloths have been mentioned so far only in passing, and as yet not at all in directly personal terms, but let me now introduce you to the rather odd notion that you have a sloth of your very own deep inside you. This will give you a bit of time to get used to the idea before we come back to sloths later on in the book. All that is needed at this stage is for you to remember that once upon a time, when you were still in touch with your sloth, you were rather better at living in the moment than you are today. There will have been times, when you were young, when you were unaware of the urgency of absolutely everything, or of the need to achieve 25 things before breakfast, and when it was enough for you to roll down a hill or notice a passing butterfly to feel happy.

With the help of our inner sloth, we still have the ability to access that simpler part of who we are, if we choose to do it. The sloth can put us back in touch with what is at the heart of living, guiding us away from the maelstrom and towards that gentler life that so many of us dream of, a life focused more on enriched moments and less on speed and consumption.

Fortunately, the sloth's time seems to have come, because the backlash against the drive to frenzied excess has started.

We can see the evidence of this in the number of high-profile business people who have down-sized in recent years – among them senior executives at BAA and Coca Cola, who said they were leaving their organisations to improve the quality of their lives and (without the usual cynical political implications) to spend more time with their families. Then there is the arrival in high-street bookshops of books with titles such as In Praise of Slow, The Joy of Laziness and Perfect Madness: Motherhood in the Age of Anxiety.

Slow Towns are being declared, such as the delightful and restful Ludlow in Shropshire, England, which is attracting the interest of people who feel that, after all, there isn't always that much more to life than stuffing a mushroom – that time might be better spent indulging directly in the sensual pleasures of preparing food than in watching someone else do it secondhand on the television, or in sitting in traffic en route to a chic bar where they'll charge you the earth to stuff a mushroom for you.

A whole generation of people who grew up to believe that life really could be infinitely perfectible, that we could have more and more choice, and that endless growth was genuinely possible, is beginning to have serious doubts.

One of the reasons for that may be that many of the people who did such a good job of persuading us that these things could ever be and that there wasn't anything that any of us couldn't do if we set our minds to it, have either crashed to earth themselves or lived lives quite at odds with the ones they promoted to the rest of us. Others have creamed off the best of what was available and left the next generation with high expectations of what they are entitled to but low probability of being able to achieve it, as well as with the necessity of living life at a pace that will, one way or another, wear them out before they are old. Surely this wasn't the meaning of progress?

This book isn't promoting idleness or a kind of back-to-basics neanderthalism; rather, in its own self-determined way, it advocates a more relaxed pace of life, one that doesn't stifle growth but allows it to happen in a more measured way. Slow growth, or SLOTH, for short.

Without a change of attitude of this kind, we will continue to run without being able to catch up with ourselves. Like the back end of those bendy buses, we are at risk of chasing our butts so hard and fast that we end up slipping our connection and whizzing forward into a time warp that returns us to the past.

If you don't think so, ask the early-risers sweating it out at gyms around the country, or try getting a seat on a rush-hour train or jaywalking across a busy junction at 7.30 in the morning.

DIARY OF A HARDWORKING LABOURER

Henry Mayhew's reports of urban deprivation in nineteenth-century London (one of the busiest, dirtiest and most squalid places in history) make great play of the long hours the poor worked, as a way of highlighting their suffering. 'Just as the church clocks are striking five ...', 'As the morning twilight came on ...' he writes, as the working classes turn out for their day. And in another great investigative report on unacceptable Victorian conditions, the Factory Commission of 1843 takes the moral high ground by hammering home the great inequality suffered by working girls like Jane Ormerod, who worked from 5 am to 9 pm with only an hour for lunch and dinner, and was 'apt to fall asleep' at work.

I'll leave you to make up your own mind as to whether the following twenty-first century working girl's, apparently freely chosen, working week is significantly less pressured.

Monday	
6 am	Get up and go for a run
6.50 am	Return from run, shower, dress
7.20 am	Drive to park-and-ride at local station, park car and walk to station
7.50 am	Train to work
8.30 am	Arrive at work and eat breakfast
11 am	Go to other office, a 10-minute walk away – team briefing for business area I work in
12.30 pm	Underground train to a working lunch with a consultant in a gentleman's club
3 pm	Team meeting
4.30 pm	Meeting with my boss all afternoon
7.30 pm	Leave work and walk to station
7.50 pm	Train home
8.30 pm	Walk to pick up car
8.45 pm	Home and prepare dinner
10.30 pm	Bed

Tuesday

6 am	Get up and shower
6.40 am	Drive to park-and-ride at local station, park car and walk to station
7.12 am	Train to work
7.45 am	Arrive at work and grab breakfast
8.50 am	Walk to other office for meeting
1 pm	Return and work through lunch at desk
7 pm	Leave work (another late one-to-one with boss, and missed kickboxing as a result)
7.20 pm	Train home
8.00 pm	Pick up car and drive home
8.30 pm	Dinner
9.30 pm	Watch telly and bed

Wednesday

5.30 am	Get up and throw on pre-prepared tracksuit
5.40 am	Leave for aerobics, park car and walk to station
6.09 am	Train eventually arrives at 6.40 am
7 am	Aerobics
8.10 am	Underground train into central London
9 am	Training all day
5.15 pm	Train home and pick up car
6.15 pm	Arrive home
7.55 pm	Dinner
10.30 pm	Fall asleep on sofa watching *Desperate Housewives*!

Thursday

6 am	Get up, put the rubbish out, shower
6.45 am	Drive to park-and-ride at local station, park car and walk to station
7.19 am	Train to London – training all day out of office
5.15 pm	Underground train
6 pm	Meet friends for drinks
8 pm	Dinner in restaurant
9.20 pm	Leave restaurant and go to station
10.20 pm	Wait 25 minutes for train
10.50 pm	Partner picks me up from the station
11.04 pm	Home and bed

Friday	
6 am	Get up and shower
6.40 am	Drive to park-and-ride at local station, park car and walk to station
7.45 am	Arrive at work
8.50 am	Leave for meeting at other office
1.20 pm	Return to main office
5.30 pm	Leave work for friend's leaving do in another part of central London
6.10 pm	Arrive at club
8 pm	Leave party and walk to station
8.50 pm	Wait half an hour for train home
9.40 pm	Home
10 pm	Dinner
Saturday	
6.50 am	Wake up ... why, why, why?
7 am	Feed cats, read and have a cup of tea
7.40 am	Clean house
10.30 am	Eat a bowl of cereal and do paperwork
1 pm	Take dry cleaning to cleaners then go to gym
8 pm	Watch telly – all rubbish
10.00 pm	Go to bed early
Sunday	
8 am	Wake and read for ages
11 am	Go to local town centre to pick up some bits and pieces
12.30 pm	Go out for lunch locally
4 pm	Come back and work for a couple of hours
6 pm	Watch telly
10.30 pm	Bed

While there are lots of social activities in among that week's hard work that Jane Ormerod could only have dreamed of, even had she been able to imagine them, there are also lots of things equally hard for her to imagine but rather less enviable: for example, the distances this modern girl has to travel just to get to work, together with the waiting times she spends at stations, which eat up hours of her life, and the self-imposed fitness regime. Jane would probably have thought the idea of *making time* to go to fitness classes a joke. In all probability,

Jane's health and fitness was her much shorter, but pedestrian, journey to work.

The week of the twenty-first-century working girl is a mixture of necessity and personal choice. Some of what she does she could choose not to do, unlike Jane Ormerod, but only if she also chooses to ignore today's cultural demands and expectations. At the same time, if she chooses to live in an urbanised area of a Western country, she has no choice but to work very hard in order to earn enough money to afford it, and that involves spending long hours simply getting herself to work as well, which in turn means she's left with little time to fit in normal amounts of just about anything else, including exercise.

All of which would make much more sense if what we were getting back from the virtually Victorian hours and effort involved in all of the above was absolutely brilliant, giving us untold advantages over those Victorian drudges. So do the educated young woman with the diary, and her partner (both of whom need to earn, of course) live it up in a mansion? No, they can just about afford to live in the same kind of tiny two-up, one-down terraced cottage that Jane Ormerod may well have lived in herself – and they would have to make all kinds of sacrifices if they were ever to have children.

We don't seem to have cracked it yet, do we? And that is why, in this book, we are turning to some creatures which, if not exactly in the vanguard of progress, have shown a tremendous ability to survive comfortably by simply hanging on in there. Sloths are remarkable in many ways, but one of the things that makes them stand out is that they have a very strong grip. Perhaps it really is time we took a few tips from them!

1

Out of our tree

Sloths don't seem to do a lot most of the time except hang around in trees, and they look so genially sleepy you can't imagine them ever being truly busy at anything but chilling out completely. Sloths just don't *do* hurry either. Yet, somehow, despite their relaxed pace and amiable ways, they still get all the necessary sloth work done, which is evident because their species has survived for millions of years. How differently nature must have set them up from us, with our addiction to speed.

Perhaps we should never have come down from the trees either.

All right, it's time to get to the point, but a little whimsy doesn't really do any harm, and perhaps it can even highlight a deeper question.

At certain stages in human development there may well be a need for us to do a survival stocktake – to take time out to ask ourselves if there is a genuine purpose behind what we are doing, or if we are doing what we do simply because we have got into the habit of doing it. For example, right now we seem to have got into the habit of speeding up both life and development inexorably, as though speed and growth are ends in themselves. Let us at least consider the proposition that if sloths can keep on making life happen without racing around like lunatics, it must be a possibility – life doesn't only happen to dynamos.

Seriously, while it is in fact pretty obvious that we evolved in quite different ways from sloths and armadillos, and that this book isn't a feeble attempt to rewrite The Origin of the Species, there may be a real case for considering whether or not we have started to make so much more effort than is needed to survive well, that we have reached the point of overkill – as though we are rubbing our hands together to warm them on a chilly night ... and ending up setting them on fire. If we no longer have to struggle in order to survive, why can't we take pleasure in simply sitting back and enjoying what we have?

Because what a lot of everything we do have. We have gadgets to perform every function for us, from washing our clothes to washing ourselves. We have ways to transport ourselves through air, across water and over land, and if we don't want to transport ourselves, we have ways of making contact with every person we've ever known, by e-mail, text or telephone. We have ways to heat our world and cool it down. There's food available to us from virtually every nation on earth; entertainment that saves us from ever having to think if we don't choose to; chemicals to make us cheerful, chemicals to bring us down, and chemicals to make the world a different place. And on top of all that, there cannot be a single personal or domestic adornment conceivable that hasn't at some stage been made available to a discerning buyer in some outlet, somewhere.

Perhaps that's why we can't really get as much enjoyment out of life as we think we should. We are back to overload. We are gobbling at the Last Chance Saloon, filling our faces with everything indiscriminately – starters, main course, desserts – so that we are not actually able to savour any of it properly. Overconsumers Anonymous.

And like addicts of every persuasion, we are in the business of doing most things to excess, from work and exercise to highs to lows – even, ironically, sometimes indolence and depression. But the real point is that we are not stopping at the middle ground of relaxed, absorbed, appreciative enjoyment. We are far too busy being on the up, or being on the down, which disturbs the overall balance. And having set the relentless pace, we are rather stuck with the consequences, which are getting passed down the generations.

We too often seem like a society of rather mixed-up, hard-working, but essentially insecure, sugar-dependent kids. In fact, it sometimes appears that many so-called advanced nations are suffering from a vast cultural case of ADHD, with millions afflicted by excessive but randomly directed zeal, rushing from cause to cause, sport to sport, lifestyle to lifestyle and panic to panic. Then there's our greed for syrupy consumption, the tendency to self-absorption and depression, and the expectation of immediate gratification in food, entertainment and relationships. We get ourselves worked up about CJD one minute, bird flu the next; we find glutinous, formulaic, soap operas more satisfying than Shakespeare; and we split up because 'I wasn't getting my needs met' as frequently as we take Prozac.

Stability is what is missing – true, engaged, confident connectedness with who we are and where we belong. If we want to slow everything down a bit and get more value from life, we will first have to learn to believe in ourselves. We need confidence; not confidence of the spin-doctor brash kind, but the sort of confidence that comes from security, the kind that will allow us to feel more relaxed in our own judgements. Without this confidence in our own instincts, we end up anxious or alienated, restlessly searching for approval or excitement and overly dependent on gratification of appetite and on other people's opinions and judgements.

WAS IT CHIPPENDALE WHO CHOPPED DOWN THE TREE?

When did we learn not to believe in ourselves? How did we became detached from authentic connections in the first place? What was the stimulus for our dependency on stimulants? And why do people have to work so hard to achieve the basics these days, while the extras seem to have become standard?

You could say it all started with design, technology and industrial production – perhaps we should blame Thomas Chippendale. Before him, when somebody *needed* a chair they sourced their tree from the local wood, dragged it home, and carved their chair in whatever style suited the timber, their taste, their way of life and their home. Of course this is a hugely simplified version of events, but I think you can see where I'm coming from. It's worth giving it a little thought.

And while you are doing that, let's go back a bit further in time to the Tudors, because they were responsible for a huge increase in travel and trade. With trade came increased wealth, and with increased wealth came the middle classes, who are clearly to blame for all manner of things, not least the revolutionising of production.

Even during Tudor times, though, most people had only as many personal and household goods as they actually needed to eat, sleep, work and so on, and those would have been produced close to home, if not in the home. The same goes, by and large, for food, which would have been locally produced for most of the population, with all the benefits and drawbacks that entailed.

Commercially speaking, after the Tudors there was a quiet time during the Civil War and the following Revolution, but then came a period of relative peace and prosperity (together with an excess, that is of Georges) and another spurt in growth of the middle classes, who exceeded their limited possessions and decided they wanted to shop (no change there, then).

And this is where things took off. Though the eighteenth century had nothing on the nineteenth in terms of conspicuous consumption, it set the ball rolling downhill by starting up the forms and means of production, which led not only to excessive demand but also to the separation of our domestic lives from our working lives. Before the eighteenth century, the only people who routinely split their working world from their domestic one were those who had to travel long distances, for example to fight or to trade. Never mind a work/life balance, most people would have had a full-on work/life inter-mix, with work as often as not taking place in the home. And if they worked on the land, it would have been a local, as well as a family, affair.

In the eighteenth century, as well as being involved in matters such as literature, science and political cartoons, the middle classes were responsible for inventing machinery, design, factories and mass production, all of which made it possible for them to shop on an industrial scale. Machinery speeded up the manufacture of an item. Design broke up the manufacturing process into individual elements (one man making many chair legs, instead of whole chairs, for example), so rendering it more efficient. Factories made it possible to manufacture several items simultaneously: mass production was the logical outcome.

To be fair to Chippendale, he wasn't exactly the eighteenth-century equivalent of Ikea. What he introduced into this burgeoning industrial equation was, simply, a pattern book. In 1754 he published the most un-industrial-sounding *The Gentleman and Cabinet Maker's Director*. The book sold around the world, and the sophisticated furniture designs in the book standardised people's expectations and made locally produced furniture seem amateur and old-fashioned by comparison. He brought consumer envy to life. And the developing factories quickly brought the identical goods within the buying power of thousands of middle-class people.

Okay, Chippendale wasn't the first person in history to produce designs that were copied by others; nor did he twist people's arms to make them prefer his styles over others. As far as I know, neither did he presume to tell people how not to furnish their houses. But he became a household name and started a trend of sorts, by showing people that they could look beyond their own home town for design inspiration and that they could be part of a national, not to say international, marketplace.

But people could only participate in that marketplace, of course, if they were middle class. Someone had to produce the goods that the middle classes were buying in larger and larger quantities, and if those goods were being produced in factories, the workers in these factories were inevitably detached from their homes a lot of the time. This meant that they were less able to produce food for themselves, make their own clothes, make their own furniture and so on. As a result, they had to buy ready-made food and goods, but since they were on very low wages they couldn't afford them, so they borrowed money and got into debt ... which they had to work longer hours to repay. And there we see some recognisable patterns involving desire, detachment, distance, production, consumption and artificiality, and a spiral of time, money, borrowing, debt ... and time again.

It might still seem a gigantic leap from Chippendale's Director to today's lifestyle gurus, but think about that word 'director'. It's a strong one, implying someone who must not only know what he or she is doing but also be sufficiently intelligent and knowledgeable to give sound advice to others, even if it's not actually about remote, professional matters but to do with the way you make personal choices in your immediate world. Of course, the director doesn't know you or your circumstances, but the implication is that he or she probably knows better. So Mr Chippendale won't consider how Aunt Betsy's favourite rocking chair will fit with his fashionable furniture; he won't cut down one of his pieces for you so it will fit below the window. No, in effect he will ask you to make all the adjustments because he is not accommodating anything to your known world; you are accommodating your world to fit his grand design.

ADRIFT IN THE WORLD

There, in a nutshell, we have the beginnings of what has become a whole way of life, one that we have become so used to that we don't question it at all. We assume that mobility, moving on, the splitting of life from work, long hours, an overwhelming amount of choice, debt, mass-produced food and goods, fancy goods themselves, all-encompassing professional design and the interventions of self-styled experts are somehow inevitable, or possibly even natural. And when people start to feel uncomfortable with having to live like this, when they lose confidence in their own experience, feel marginalised or find the pace of life too fast, rather than trusting their own reactions they are likely to turn to artificial stimulants such as alcohol, sugar or drugs to blank out the sensations, provide comfort, and give themselves more energy and drive. But this energy and drive is hyperactive: noisy, aimless and greedy for more.

In becoming reliant on outside supplies of everything, from food and heat to opinions on taste, we have lost touch with reality. How else could so many people believe that an unlimited number of us can have anything we want. What if we all want to be the next President of the United States? Becoming detached from the security of what we have known has made us desperate to find security in new beliefs and left us very uncertain of our own capacity for judgement, as well as persuadable to the point of gullibility. In fact, we've become so unsure of ourselves and our right to own our own experiences that we've allowed ourselves to be virtually infantilised by the self-help industry and pathologised by experts.

There have always been people prepared to inflate and live off other people's neuroses – that's what *Othello* is all about. Snake-oil salesmen have a long history; and, as we've seen, design consultants have a lengthy track record too. But what's happening now is in another league, and it seems to be turning half of us into inadequate, narcissistic clones.

Of course, the great ratcheting up is partly a result of exposure. With the explosion of media sources – TV, radio, newspapers, text messaging, the internet, glossy magazines, Sunday supplements – we are subject to constant spin doctoring, marketing, quackery, persuasion, the hard sell – call it what you will – and that puts those of us who are the most uncertain of all in a very vulnerable position. Because every day it benefits some new special interest group or individual to persuade us that we are inadequate, or imperfect, often in every possible way.

꒦ Does your house need a makeover?

꒦ ... ...ealth?

꒦ ... ...e attention?

꒦ ... ...hose clothes?

🍌 Isn't it time you did something about your body?

🍌 What state is your mind in?

If you respond to any of these questions by feeling that you are not quite up to scratch, you have already fallen victim. The implication is that whoever you are and however you live, there's something wrong with it – but the expert can put it right.

Of course, in order to put it right, they first have to make it wrong, and they do this by pathologising normal. This insidious and opportunistic drive is, at least, being challenged by some people still well enough connected to their own sense of reality to see through the duplicity. According to the authors of a new book, *One Nation Under Therapy*, the happier Americans get, the more they are showing up on the therapist's couch. While, according to a recent Gallup poll, 88 per cent of the US population report themselves as happier than ever before, yet they are turning to therapy in increasing numbers in order to 'boost their self-esteem' and develop 'emotional intelligence'. Rather than get *genuinely* in touch with themselves and discover that, at heart, they are pretty well off, they depend instead on gurus, who tell them they are in pretty bad shape.

If you ask someone whether they are feeling well or if they are happy with their body shape – surprise, surprise – they begin to wonder, 'Am I?' A glossy magazine finds that 95 per cent of women are unhappy with their bodies – well, fancy that. Set up the question and you set up the doubt. If we are disconnected from our certainties and preyed on by people who want something from us, isn't it only too easy to feel we must be in the wrong? If you want to make money out of people, first generate uncertainty.

You'd be amazed at just what people are prepared to believe once they have suspended their own judgement in favour of yours. If you have any doubt about that, you need only look at the number of people who have become so mindlessly dependent on their sat-nav to do their thinking for them that they would probably drive through hell if they were told to. The god of irony must have been watching, for in the wonderfully named English village of Crackpot, in Yorkshire, drivers have been known to drive up a dirt track to the edge of a cliff with a 30-metre drop, despite all the sensory evidence that should have made them think at least 20 times before going there. Likewise, in the English village of Luckington, Wiltshire, cars have been driven on into a ford marked 'unsuitable for motor vehicles', and deep enough in to swamp both driver and car. Is that worried-looking driver who is cruising along your cul de sac right now really trying to find the M1?

The problem with sat-navs, as with a lot of the other sources of help and information that we turn to today, is that they are so generic, so universal, that they can no more apply to us personally than a two-line horoscope for Aquarians. Does 'You will have a windfall this week' mean that every single Aquarian is in line to win the big prize on the Lotto? Surely not.

Whatever the drawbacks, such as gossip and loss of privacy, that came with turning to those who knew you best for assistance in days gone by, at least the help or advice they gave would have been specific and relevant, and at best it might have been given with a sympathetic awareness of all the human issues involved in your situation:

> Don't worry, love. Your dad doesn't mean it when he says he couldn't care less what you do. He's dead proud of you really, always telling everyone in the pub how well you're doing. You've got to remember he had a tough childhood himself. He was left to bring himself up – never learnt to talk about things. Perhaps you expect too much of him.

Today, if you take your issues to an agony aunt, the reply is more likely to sound like this:

> University is a big step and you have a right to expect consideration from your family. If your father won't discuss this, I suggest you ask him if he will join you in seeing a family therapist. You need to open up with each other.

Which brings us back to the problem of ordering our world to fit into someone else's grand design.

KAYLEIGH AND CUMAWAIN

Whatever happened to lives and to living? We don't seem to have those any more, we all seem to have lifestyles instead. We ditch all the bits and pieces that have accumulated while we have been living and replace them, wholesale, with a lifestyle look. Do you ever wonder what people do, after the cameras have moved on from the *Reinvent Your Home*-type house, with the ridiculed things that Granny and Mum and Great-aunt Mimi saved so hard for and lovingly polished? Do they furtively pull them out again? Do they put the crinoline doll back on the loo roll, the photo of Uncle Jack, killed in 1939, back on the sideboard, and the carved love-spoon back on the wall, or can they actually bring themselves to auction them off as a job lot (when as like as not they'll be snapped up by a chain of theme pubs)?

And do people ever really *live* like that, in their newly reinvented 'home' – with horizontal bands of immaculate throws over their beds, surgical gowns around their chairs, and artfully grouped pebbles and twigs on their tables? Would most of us have come up with solutions like those by ourselves? Surely not!

Equally bizarre and artificial is the fashion for lifestyle names for kids that is trickling down from image-conscious celebrities to us humbler mortals. Why don't more of us want to celebrate our roots nowadays by using names that our families have used? Instead we take our lead from distant personalities, who choose reference names that have more to do with *zeitgeist* than with taste or sense. How else did a Tom and Katie come up with a Suri, a David and Victoria with a Brooklyn, a Gwyneth and Chris with an Apple? How will it sound when they call out to their kids in the park? 'Come along, Apple, Mummy's got an apple for you'?

And where the great lead, the rest will follow, registering their little ones Kayleigh, Chardonnay, Chelsea and the like. But are all these names truly hip and culturally inspired breaks with tradition, or are they just the modern human equivalent of house names such as Cumawain, Dunroamin, Mafeking and Mandalay? We should always be aware of what the future might think, and that includes our future children. How thankful are they going to be for the strange names we are lumbering them with? What sort of chameleon world are we creating for them?

Having taken on board the general impression that the past we inherited was pretty imperfect and inadequate, that so are we, and that the only way we can be made better is by learning from people who are much more perfect than ourselves, we now seem to be happily prepared to take advice from them on just about every subject imaginable. The advice itself has to be regularly updated and inflated, as do the experts. We feel an urgent need to keep on our toes and avoid falling back into the dangerous pit of lethargy, of routine, of conformity with the old. We must keep moving towards the heights of perfection – *avanti*!

I recently counted 220 self-help and lifestyle (i.e. life change) magazines racked shelf over shelf in one large supermarket. Buy your decor with your bread and peas, your body and your mental stability with your cereals.

Why live in a suburban semi when, with a few metres of tulle and a purple and gold makeover, you can turn it into an exotic seraglio; why make do with a top-floor flat when, by quickly ripping the ceiling out, you can turn it into a state-of-the-art urban space? If only every TV makeover presenter or magazine editor had to pay for the repairs to relationships when inspired amateurs think they can carry out change as quickly or as glossily as they do in the shots. Once again, it's all about separating ourselves from the reality of our own experience and buying into a totally unlikely, manufactured or culturally remote fantasy.

One of the bestselling home-improvement magazines on the shelves unself-consciously writes text like this:

> When Flappy came to decorate the enfilade of downstairs rooms, she was determined to 'listen' to the house.

Wherever are they coming from? But, more to the point, wherever are they taking us, if we're gullible enough to follow them?

As if it's not bad enough that we inflict weird names and strange decor on kids who would probably be happier to be called Tom and Jenny and to live in a house that had a dog and smelt of cooking, we inflict greater horrors still on the dogs themselves. Even they, poor accommodating creatures, are now being turned into style accessory freaks. Of course, there have been pink dogs and dogs subjected to the indignities of docking and topiary clipping for ages. Now, though, sad people watch TV shows about other sad people who need to dress dogs like teenage glamour models and treat them like tricky film stars, and they see nothing wrong in copying them. Then they wonder why their dogs lose their doggy identity and pack-based behaviour and start to act like incontinent prima donnas, who are probably called Paris.

MAKING LIFE OVER

Before being tempted to copy what we see on the television, we should at least first recognise that everything on the screen is fake or fudged, and then we will only have ourselves to blame for the messes we get into. After all, nobody went into the television business primarily to improve the world; people go into it to make a living. Now, if they did it for free ...

On one well-known UK TV programme about property development, the developer was asked the 'actual cost' of the work involved. What the audience didn't know was that, for complex personal tax reasons, he had no intention of sharing an accurate cost, so when he gave his answer to camera he lied. Fair enough, that's between him and the taxman – and about eight million other people, of whom only one per cent has to be gullible enough to believe him for 80,000 people potentially to be vulnerable to risking everything they have on a similar 'profit-making' venture.

It is clearly not in the interests of making watchable (and therefore profitable) television to put all sorts of disclaimers into a property-developing format. No, the disclaimers will come in a *Watchdog*-style programme. But life for real people just doesn't come in separate categories like that; we have to cover all the ground simultaneously.

Television producers, though, can shift reality about however they choose. Remember those cardboard cut-out dolls that come with interchangeable sets of clothes, and even characters? Making a TV programme is a bit like that. They place different heads on different sets of clothes. For one woman who got involved in the making of an item on a local television news programme this came as a bit of a surprise. She thought she had been giving a talk to a group of people she knew and later chatting about it with a pleasant interviewer who made normal, sensible responses. When she watched the film of the same event on television later that day, she discovered it must have been a quite different experience!

What she saw on the screen was that she had been giving the talk not to the fairly ordinary and rather homely collection of people she knew but, in fact, to a different set of people completely: a very smart and together group of suits. No longer was her audience sitting in a small grey office; they had been transported to a much more impressive and well-lit auditorium. Meanwhile, the interviewer was coming back at her with slick, knowledgeable comments and making knowing nods to the audience throughout.

Her first thought was 'Why? Just why?' and perhaps we should all ask that question too. It was a very little item, on a very local news programme; why adjust it? Why tell such visual and verbal lies? What could the purpose possibly be when it was a news item, not a self-improvement show?

I want to come back to the question of the credibility of media commentators, experts and gurus later, but in the meantime there is once again the business of authenticity. If we don't trust our own perceptions, if we don't stop, look and listen for ourselves, we're more likely to be up for the sort of pre-hashed, re-shaped turkey twizzler lives that UK TV cook Jamie Oliver has taken apart in culinary terms.

AND WHY HOUSES GOT MORE EXPENSIVE BECAUSE OF MR CHIPPENDALE

Near the beginning of this chapter I made the rather curious claim that Thomas Chippendale was responsible for how we live now, and I went on to list the ways in which eighteenth- and nineteenth-century means of production led to people's lives becoming detached and driven – ways that have become even more extreme today. I noted that, like us, people back then worked too hard, borrowed a lot of money and got into debt. I also noted that at least at that time the housing was cheap. Why should this be? Why should housing have been relatively cheap right up to the 1960s, while technical goods and machinery were expensive, whereas now it's the other way round? On this question, I'm going to make another curious claim – because we are as far off from seeing a house for what it is these days as we are from seeing the reality behind a TV programme or, for some of us, the dogginess of a dog.

That's because we have become detached from a basic functional relationship with our homes. When homes stopped being places where working life went on for at least half the population, where food was manufactured (i.e. grown and cooked) and the greater part of people's lives simply happened, then prices started to go up. In the past, even the poorest of rural peasants, if they had some kind of work, could afford to live somewhere. Now, even the poorest of people seem to be able to afford a satellite dish, but some of the better-off in London can't run to a home, even if they work a long day.

For a lot of reasons and in many ways, a house has stopped being seen simply as somewhere to live and become instead another lifestyle option, investment opportunity, television makeover target, design statement, production line outcome, backdrop space for acting out against, marketing opportunity, pension plan, tax fiddle, divorce bargaining tool, inheritance, container of consumer goods, hobby, target for the planners, politicians, taxman. It's just another heavily sold product, and as such is compared with other products and found to be more valuable.

Which is why Mr Chippendale is responsible for housing costing us so much. His *Director* sold us on the notion that we could design our world from a distance, and produce it in bits and pieces. It persuaded us that we didn't have to take our lead from the past but could detach and arrange things according to new trends, a process that has escalated so fast that the idea that your life will be the same as your parents', more or less, been almost completely lost in a generation. Of course, things weren't ever really as static as all that, but the pace of change was more subtle, less in your face.

LET'S SLOTH IT ALL DOWN

As I said earlier on, I am putting the case for slowing the pace down again, not for bringing it to a complete standstill, nor for all of us simply lying around in total indolence. This book is an argument for the rediscovery of the lost art of living, which is a (now rather eroded) foundation for any balanced human society.

- We need to be more adaptive to our environment and less driven by artificial and costly forces, such as media pressure and 'expert' advice.

- We need to slow our lives down to a more leisurely pace, letting go of the attachment to unsustainable over-achievement that has led to such high stress levels, as well as to addictive over-consumption of just about everything.

- We need not to have to be perfect, which means not being exposed, whether we like it or not, to unrealistic media images that make us feel inadequate.

- We need to own our own experience and to be allowed to believe the evidence of our eyes, ears and understanding rather more, so that we are relieved of the pressure to be someone else and can simply be who we are.

- We need to enjoy living in the moment a whole lot more, rather than trying to live in the future perfect.

- We need to be able to sit back from time to time and enjoy the serene contemplation of the rich memories we have accumulated from those moments – possibly with a small glass of something special.

Ironically, a lot of us have become so unused to this way of living that we may actually need to turn to the experts to rediscover it. So who can we look to to model this way of life? Not to television personalities or film stars, not to style gurus, and certainly not to the inhabitants of glossy magazines.

No, we need to go to the zoo. There we will find a gloriously relaxed, measured, adaptive, natural, economical, tolerant, gently paced creature that will ask nothing of us at all, but simply swing from its tree and gently smile.

Say hello to the sloth.

2

Just hanging around

Sloths are absolutely amazing creatures, and they have a pretty amazing fan base, too. Look them up on the internet and you'll find 750,000 websites that refer to them! One of these, www.geo cities.com/hollywood/set/1478/sloth.html, is guaranteed to put a genial, sloth-like smile on the face of anyone who logs on to it. It would be a sad soul who couldn't be made merrier by discovering this site celebrating the wonderful, wonderful sloth. The sloth's time is coming – be patient; it will be worth waiting for.

The name sloth actually means slow-moving, that's all, so how has it come to connote lazy? Sloths are not lazy; they work just as hard as is necessary to conduct the business of their lives – and no more. That's one of the great joys of these brilliantly adapted creatures, that they are economical of effort, and it is among the most significant things we can learn from them if we want more relaxed lives ourselves.

If one of the most important pieces of business of any creature's life is survival, then sloths have done pretty well so far, so we can hardly say they have been slouches when it comes to carrying out the essentials. Sloths go back to the Ice Age, and they are such a successful species that in parts of South and Central America, where they mostly live, they make up as much as two-thirds of what biologists call 'the mammalian biomass'. In other words, there are more of them than there are members of the other species in their habitat by quite a long way. In fact, they've been successful enough to see off a lot of the busy, chatteringly hyperactive monkey species in some places.

How on earth have they managed this? How has the slowest animal on earth, one that rarely moves faster than a remarkably relaxed 0.5 kilometres an hour and can sleep up to 20 hours a day, managed to achieve such a result? The following extract from an e-mail to the sloth website mentioned above (one of many quite bizarre but nevertheless highly entertaining offerings) could well hit the nail on the head:

The three-toed sloth is not well informed about the outside world.

Another way of putting that would be to say that the sloth is dedicated to taking care of itself and doesn't waste a lot of its essential resources in bothering about things too far from home.

So how has the sloth pulled off the whole survival business without bothering about the outside world anything like as much as the rest of us, while at the same time retaining its legendary level of cool? To answer this question, we need to take a more detailed look at the sloth's way of life, considering its unique approach to such issues as defence, competition, reproduction, consumption, toilet habits and so on – in other words, at all the things that make the sloth, quite simply, the sloth.

THE SLOTH HABITAT

Sloths live in the rain forests of Central and South America. They spend most of their lives in the trees, hanging upside-down from the branches. Three-toed sloths (there are two-toed sloths, too, but the three-toed variety is the one we are mostly interested in) are 'active' both day and night, and will move, perhaps daily, from one tree to another, but nearly always sideways, from branch to branch, hand over hand, rather than going down one tree and up another. They tend to have a fairly narrow stamping ground, but can cover greater distances during floods, because they happen to be rather good swimmers.

Their shaggy coats camouflage them as they hang motionless in the trees, looking more like bunches of dried leaves than anything living, which helps protect them from attack. When hanging around in palm trees (among their favourites) they clearly feel they can take some small pride in occasionally being mistaken for coconuts.

THE PHYSICAL ATTRIBUTES OF THE SLOTH

Sloths, which grow to the size of a cat or small dog, weighing about 6 kilograms, have some unusual but eco-friendly physical features. They have a sweet-natured, apparently smiling face, with a rather fetching dark mask around the eyes, but the rest of their appearance (and smell) is more compost heap than matinee idol. Their scruffy-looking long grey or brown fur, despite what you might think to the contrary, is groomed daily, but has a greenish tinge, caused by the algae that grow along tiny grooves in the hair in the rainy season. Though this makes for great camouflage – and, as caterpillars live off the algae, a great eco-system too – the overall effect is distinctly Wurzel Gummidge.

Another less attractive but useful defence feature is the sloth's toes, which are long, curving and clawed, and can clamp themselves around branches. This means that even if sloths get attacked they can still hang on in there, which adds to the difficulties of whatever beast is trying to attack them.

The last curiosity of their appearance is the incredible flexibility of their joints, which allows them to turn their heads right round like owls, and enables them to reach for leaves from every direction without having to take the trouble to move.

REPRODUCTION AND OTHER SUCH MATTERS

A normal sloth lifespan in the wild is about 10 to 20 years, although granddaddies of up to 40 years old have been known in captivity.

The males are solitary creatures, while the females hang around in groups. It is not clear how selection of partners is made, but sex seems to take place, upside-down as ever, in whatever tree the female is found in. Females mature at three years and have offspring at the end of six-month pregnancies every year after that. The babies are tiny (25 cm), unbearably cute, and stay with their mothers for six months, being carried about on the fur and at six weeks weaned onto leaves. When the baby reaches six months old, one day the mother simply leaves it, by continuing to move on as she grazes. Up until then, the baby will always keep at least one foot on her as it reaches out for its own leafy supplies. The relationship between mother and child is hardly an over-protective one, though, since if the baby takes a nose-dive out of the tree, the mother is more likely than not to leave it where it lands!

FOOD AND ANY OTHER BUSINESS

The sloth eats shoots and leaves, but it doesn't regularly punctuate using the colon!

Seriously, sloths eat a huge variety of leaves, most of which are fairly indigestible, as well as often poisonous, so they have to have an incredibly slow metabolism to allow the food to be processed gradually and harmlessly through the gut. A process that usually takes hours for other animals takes from a week to a month for a sloth, which therefore only needs to go to the loo every eight days or so. It doesn't need to drink at all, because it gets all its liquid from the slow digestion of the greenery it consumes.

It appears that as the mother sloth carries her baby around, she teaches it to have a particular preference both for certain types of leaves and for certain territories (matrilineal inheritance, okay Germaine?), so each sloth family targets slightly different trees from the others, thus reducing competition.

One of the main occasions for a sloth to come down from its tree is to take a dump, which it does after digging a hole for it at the foot of its tree. It then buries the evidence and climbs back up again. One theory is that this forms a kind of nutritional recycling, as the sloth is fertilising its own particular food source.

A RELAXED METABOLISM

The sloth's metabolism is v ... e ... r ... y slow. Not only does food go through the system slowly, but every other internal process of the sloth is equally relaxed. As a result of this economy of effort, its core body temperature is more variable than that of other animals, going up or down according to outside conditions. Sloths adapt to their world, and as nights can get cold in the rainforest, rather than rush about warming themselves through effort, they simply spend the night inside the leaf canopy and then go up to the surface in the morning. There they spread themselves out, belly up, and let the sun take the strain, as they warm themselves all the way through.

COMPETITION – WHAT COMPETITION?

Because sloths eat only greenery, their main competitors would logically be monkeys and reptiles. It seems, however, that they have seen off most monkeys because monkeys are a lot more fussy about what they'll eat. And whereas many reptiles compete with others of their species for the same food source, sloths, with their different individual preferences for particular leaf species, don't compete with their own neighbours and so can keep their larders well stocked. As a species, they are very flexible food-wise, but individually they source locally and uncompetitively.

SAFETY IN THE TREETOPS

Despite their lack of speed, sloths don't have many enemies. As we have already noted, their symbiotic relationship with algae protects them very effectively from being spotted as they hang, foliage-like, in the rain forest canopy.

The sloth's main threat probably comes from human beings destroying their environment. They do have a select few predators, however. They are vulnerable to jaguars and harpy eagles, and sometimes have to fight off certain smaller predators, such as weasels and cats. Competitive young males also occasionally have to fight off one another. Although they are slow to rouse, sloths have very nasty claws. The following description of a sloth Waterloo is by Jacalyn Giacalone (you can find if at http://rainforest.montclair.edu/pwebrf/rainforest/Animals/mammals/sloths.html):

> I have seen a three-way fight among three male three-toes. They first called to each other from about 50 metres apart with loud high-pitched screaming sounds. The sloths approached each other at top speed – for sloths – and then engaged in slashing, arm-swinging battles. One male fell from the tree to the ground, about 25 metres. Stunned but apparently unharmed, he soon began the process of climbing the nearest sapling and scanning his surroundings, finally reaching for lianas that would get him back up to the canopy.

So although the sloth's defence systems mostly consist of camouflage, as a last resort it is still quite capable of giving as good as it gets. The sloth is a tough and thick-skinned animal. Just as it can digest quite toxic stuff without harm, so it can deal with nasty falls and injuries without making too much of the hurt. Sloths pick themselves up, dust themselves down and start all over again.

AND THIS IS GOOD BECAUSE?

While the three-toed sloth is not well informed about the outside world, the outside world has never been particularly well informed about the three-toed sloth either, and this sloth-like transmission of information seems to have worked quite well for the sloth.

By sticking to a way of life that keeps things local, low-profile and slow, sloths can afford not to bother themselves too much with externals, which would only put them at risk of becoming someone's dinner anyway. So unless they feel the need to bask in the sun for a bit, they spend most of their time just hanging around, being legendarily cool.

3

What the sloth can do for us

As even the most laid-back of humans goes faster than 0.5 kph and is unlikely to encourage the growth of green slime in their hair, it would clearly be more than absurd to suggest that there could ever be more than a passing similarity between the two species. We have houses, mortgages, cars, politics, newspapers, nuclear warheads, and usually pick our kids up when they fall down, so our circumstances and requirements are quite different from the sloth's. No, I'm certainly not advocating that we try to make ourselves over as another species, but when it comes to pace of life, the sloth has an awful lot to teach us.

Up to now, our pace of life has been set by the human desire for growth, which has been partly driven by the threats we were up against in the distant past, when shaggy things with teeth played a large part in our nightmares. We have had to stay on the move in order to defend ourselves, and to roam around looking for better places to be in than our neighbours. So movement and growth have, historically, been pretty essential to the survival and development of the human species, even though the pace of both has been rather less frenetic than it is today. Now, though, things are changing so fast that we could be at risk of achieving the direct opposite of what we have been used to expect from change. Everybody knows about the threat of the global greenhouse and nuclear winter, but what about other threats, such as to the quality of the life we are living. If 'progress' is precluding enjoyment for so many ostensibly successful people, what has all the progress to date been for?

I talked to a cross-section of people living near me, in south-west England (source what you can close to home), and asked them for their thoughts on life. These are people who have everything previous generations struggled for – accommodation, heating, light, good clothes, transport, free education and the rest. Although most of them, had they been asked directly, would almost certainly have acknowledged how lucky they were to have so many of these things we now view as essentials, they didn't dwell on any enjoyment they gained from them; instead they talked about worrying themselves silly over the following subjects:

- **The environment:** The big question here is whether there will be anything left for our children once we've had all we are 'entitled' to – the irony not being lost on anyone that while we expect quite sophisticated things (computers, foreign foods and so on) to be available to us as basics, we still wish to preserve enough of nature's goodies to pass on to our children. Trying to balance this equation leads to nightmares.

- **Carbon footprints:** This is much like the above but with more detail, as in, 'If we fly to Lanzarote twice a year, run an SUV and have a hot tub on the decking, will the children be able to use more than a single 40-watt light bulb in ten years' time?' and 'Why do recycling vans leave their engines running?'

- **The school run:** A concern for concerned parents. How green can your credentials be if you drive your kids a short distance to the local school, but how can you protect them properly against today's threats if you leave them adrift on the dangerous streets of your city?

- **Defence:** If Iran has the bomb, will it be better to hunker down in Wiltshire or in the Languedoc?

- **Food:** Is there anything left that we can eat that won't make us fat, put us at risk of a stroke, or use up the resources of Kenya and leave a size 20 carbon footprint?

- **Dietary problems:** Is there any solution to IBS (from which 10–20 per cent of Westerners suffer at any one time, disproportionately female and young), without leaving every possible nutrient out of the diet and spending half one's life with – and income on – a stress counsellor?

- **Eating disorders:** Who or what is responsible for anorexia and bulimia, and why has food become such an issue that some people won't eat at all, and others can't stop?

- **Hypochondria:** On top of all the stress about genuine illnesses, such as cancer and heart disease (which are prevalent and rising in incidence), there is also illness caused by the stress felt at the possibility of illness, as in, 'I saw a dead pigeon in the park yesterday, and today I've got the most awful headache; could it be bird flu?'

- **Crime:** This goes hand in hand with concern about addiction: 'What is the point of working hard all your life if some waster high on drugs just takes it all away?'

- **Sleep:** Nobody complains about getting too much sleep – ever. Many people complain of being tired all the time.

- **Time:** There isn't enough of this to get everything that has to be done, done (and there's just so much to do). Then there's the question of having enough time left to build up a pension, because there's going to be an awfully long time not earning.

- **Depression:** Nothing would matter so much if there was any possibility of anything mattering in the first place. Depression is a regular feature of modern life. It comes with having too much to do, too little to do – and babies.

- **Careers:** If the people who are happiest in their jobs are hairdressers, cooks, beauticians and plumbers (which is the case according to a 2005 UK survey), what on earth is the point of spending all that money, time and effort in getting a degree? Then there's the issue of the quickest possible route to earning enough money to retire on? Will it be share dealing or property dealing?

None of these things would have worried a caveman very much. They are worries that result from most of us in the West having too much of just about everything and wanting to do, or achieve, much too much, much too fast.

WHEN LESS IS MORE

Here is where the sloth can be a very good role model, because the sloth, despite – or perhaps because of – being slow and not asking for too much, still survives very satisfactorily as a species and gives every impression of enjoying being what it is. Perhaps – if we are prepared to take five and look at what it is we are working for and what we are getting out of it – we can learn something quite revolutionary from the long-lived and contented sloth. That lesson is that to get more out of life, sometimes you have to put that little bit less in.

So, having looked at some fascinating information about the sloth in the previous chapter, it's now time to put the various aspects of the sloth's physical development, behaviour and environment together and translate it into a set of human attitudes and beliefs that will help us to be less driven and more accepting of the world on the world's terms, rather than ours. This will have the very delightful by-product of giving us more freedom to enjoy the full potential of each moment of our lives in a way that many of us, with our endless activities and anxieties, seem unable to do at the moment.

THE SLOTH AT ONE WITH ITS WORLD

A sloth would be a business guru's worst nightmare. Imagine the following interview, set some time in pre-history:

> Guru: *So what you're saying is that there are no tender shoots available at this location, right? This looks to me like a supply chain problem. What we need now are solutions, solutions, solutions!*

> Sloth: *Hey, no problem. I thought with time I might just learn how to digest what's right here anyway.*

Rather than worry themselves silly about what to do to change their environment, sloths had the sense to adapt. They developed complex stomachs that allowed them to process what was readily to hand. First lesson from the sloth:

> *If you don't see problems everywhere, you don't have to rush around looking for solutions.*

That is the source of the great adaptability of the sloth, which has allowed it to live contentedly off what it finds around it, rather than constantly having to set off on risky colonising expeditions or compete with other creatures for the choicest foods available.

Adaptability is only one of many, many advantages that, unlikely as it seems, the sloth has over us poor stressed-out humans. Here is a rundown of other sloth attributes that we could surely learn to adapt for ourselves.

Sloths don't get unnecessarily stressed or waste energy resources

- They preserve the greater part of their energy for their most important basic functions.
- They make their fastest progress in their most supportive environment, water, but elsewhere they take things at a steady, and energy-efficient pace.
- They are able to make speedy(ish) progress when they are threatened, but don't waste resources by rushing unnecessarily towards aggravation.
- Their flexibility of diet allows them to economise on journeys for food.
- They regulate their temperature and metabolism naturally by lying in the sun!

Sloths don't obsess about grooming

- They take care of personal hygiene but let nature play its part.

Sloths don't overstimulate themselves with additives or activity, and they sleep very well

- Perhaps rather obvious!

Sloths are very flexible physically and temperamentally

- And they can relax completely.

Sloths are not fussy about food and source it locally

- They never travel far for their meals and are very adaptable.
- They don't compete with other sloths for food.
- They eat unrefined food that releases energy slowly. They chew and digest it slowly and carefully, getting all the nutrition they can out of it and wasting hardly anything.

What the sloth can do for us

- As they get all their nutritional needs met by their diet, they have a perfect internal economy and no apparent digestive problems.

Sloths are into natural, ecologically friendly disposal of waste

- They bury their very limited by-products, which, being natural, decompose and provide compost for new growth.

Sloths don't envy or compete

- Since they aren't competing for the same foods, there is harmony within the group.
- They are not greedy and don't overgraze, so there's enough food to go around.
- They don't really want what other species have.

Sloths aren't showy

- This means they don't attract predators.
- They don't have to waste energy resources in displays of aggression, running away, or gaining the upper hand and taking from other creatures.

Sloths are peaceful

- They are not an aggressive species, but if they are attacked they have sharp claws that they are quite ready to use to defend themselves.

Sloths have thick skins

- They can tolerate hurts and poisons without needing to self-medicate and lick their wounds.
- They can take quite significant tumbles, but being physically flexible they will pick themselves up and climb right back into their tree.

Sloths don't over-protect their young

- They let the young detach gradually as they become more self-sufficient, and then they let go.
- They allow the young to take risks, and they live with the consequences.

Sloths rely on their closest group members for support

- They learn from those nearest to them, who have common interests and experiences.
- They focus on their group rather than the world beyond and don't invade other territory.

Sloths are quite remarkably contented

- They tuck their heads into their bodies and swing from their branches without appearing to be constantly on their guard or in need of charging off in pursuit of who knows what.

Sloths simply are what they are and don't keep on reinventing and rearranging themselves

- In other words, sloths appear to be at one with themselves in ways that we can only envy.

ACCENTUATE THE POSITIVE

As I said at the beginning of this chapter, this book is not a plea for us to do a most unsloth-like thing and reinvent ourselves; rather it is a promise: that if we get back in touch with the sloth-like part of ourselves – the part that happy children are familiar with but that adults seem to lose; the part that can feel enchantment in a small discovery, or contentment in lying on the grass watching a tiny world at work – then we can drop many of our current worries about what we don't have, and start to feel more enjoyment of what we do.

To return to the worriers in the straw poll on page 44, if they spent more time generally feeling glad of what they had and less time colonising other people's worries, wouldn't they be more relaxed and less unwell – and, bottom line, would it make a *huge* amount of difference to any of the things they perceive as problems?

I'm not for a minute suggesting that we chuck out all the advantages that previous generations worked so hard to provide us with; for a start that would be most ungrateful and it would also be most unlikely to appeal to anyone as an idea. This is about slower growth, not nil growth; it's about making more of the things that we do have, savouring them and appreciating their value to us, rather than messing about endlessly trying to improve them (which only eats up world resources anyway).

Nothing is ever going to be absolutely perfect, and even if it were, how great would the benefits of perfection be? For example, most of us in the Western world now have washing machines. Is that enough to make us count our blessings? No, we would rather worry about bird flu or the risk of nuclear war. If washing machines achieve an even greater degree of perfection – perhaps so that they collect our washing for us, dry it, iron it and lay it back on our shelves – won't that just give us the time and mental space to worry about the possibility of earthworms suffering from strimmer-induced stress and the effect that this might have on harvests?

Imagine the world of our great-grandmothers, who had no washing machines at all. Imagine that, instead of dumping a mixed bag of dirty togs into a box in the corner of your centrally heated kitchen and then pouring in a small amount of carefully balanced soap powder that can somehow sort reds from yellows and lycra from cotton, then closing the door and having a beer while the box and the National Grid do the work for you, you have to do it all yourself.

Imagine that you have to gather up a week's dirty linen (and don't forget it will have been worn longer and for more physical labour, so it will be much dirtier than we are used to), and then sort it into items that need soaking and those that don't. Then you have to take it into the outhouse and start the lengthy process. You soak and hand-scrub clothes that have collars, cuffs or stains, using a bar of hard soap, a scrubbing brush (no rubber gloves) and a washboard. You work till your fingers are sore and all the dirty marks are gone. You fill the copper, boil the water so the outhouse is a great steamy swamp, put in all the clothes that will fit (you'll need several goes) and keep stirring them with the wooden tongs. We won't go into dolly blue. You pull out the great sodden weight from time to time to check its progress, then when it's clean, put it into the sink and start the rinsing process – which goes on until the water is clear. You drag the clothes apart and try to fold them so that wringing won't crease them up too much, then with one hand push them, one by one, through the wringer, using the other hand to turn the wheel (at the same time trying not to let the sheets drag on the floor and get filthy). You pile the wash into a great basket and hope the weather's dry. If not, your home will be a damp and chilly place for several days. And then you'll have to iron.

Now just think, we don't have to do that. Isn't it absolutely wonderful!

CURING THE GROWTH ADDICTION

It's all a question of slowly digesting our blessings, just as the sloth digests leaves. Which takes us back to where we came in, because at the moment our society is cursed with an addiction to excess consumption and speed, which not only makes many of us far too wizzy to sit back, digest and enjoy things thoroughly, but also condemns our world to endless and unhealthy growth. It has become almost a given that growth is good, but gardeners and cancer surgeons know only too well that when the growth of some things gets out of hand, it results in destruction. If we want to cure ourselves of the addiction that leads to this kind of growth, like any addict, first we'll have to recognise that we have a problem and then we'll have to go cold turkey. It's once we've stopped using our favourite substances that we'll be in a condition to realise they weren't all they were cracked(!) up to be.

The sloth can help us through this process by showing us what it takes to lead a slower, more relaxed and holistic kind of life, and by looking so damned amused and laid-back we'd be fools not to want to give it a go ourselves.

4

Sloth help v self-help

In 1946, a middle-aged American doctor wrote a book that changed the world for a lot of people. The book was called *Baby and Child Care*, and the doctor was Benjamin Spock. In the introduction to my copy it says:

> Out of his extensive experience (and as the father of two children) Dr Spock wrote the book which has since become the greatest bestseller since bestseller lists began.

And the book begins:

> You know more than you think you do.

It goes on to tell the reader not to take what their neighbours tell them about childcare too seriously, nor what the 'experts' tell them either, but that it's all right to trust their own instincts and to follow their doctor's directions. So that's okay, then. They already know enough by instinct, but they will still need to follow a doctor's advice.

And what are the directions given by this particular doctor? Well, they run to a modest 523 pages in paperback, and generally give quite sensible advice about kids, warmth and kindliness that could well have been given by any doting granny. For example:

> We know for a fact that the natural loving care that kindly parents give their children is a hundred times more valuable than their knowing how to pin a nappy on just right or how to make a feed expertly.

For the rest, the advice is pretty much of its time, and by now a lot of it is as dated as the advice in any of the previous books on childcare that Dr Spock was taking a pop at. All the same, Spock had a tremendous influence on millions of people. Never mind their instincts (which, half the time, is just another word for stuff you learn very early on from copying those around you), most people did what the good doctor told them to do – partly because he was a doctor, but mainly because he was in print.

Noel Coward once said, 'Strange how potent cheap music is', and a similar thing could be said for cheap print. *People believe what they read if it is published.* In fact, despite what many of us fondly believe, we all tend to believe a lot more of what we read, hear and watch if it comes from the professional media than if it comes from the world immediately around us. When Dr Spock told parents to trust their instincts, what he was really advising them to do, perhaps without realising, was to place more trust in what came down to them by osmosis than in what came to them from such sources as the professional media. Had he already discovered his inner sloth? Well, perhaps partly, but certainly not entirely. Because, of course, he was himself offering an external, professional, source of advice.

So are we right to trust the 'experts'? Despite setting himself up as one of them, Dr Spock says we are not, and perhaps his own life provides the proof of the pudding, because, in spite of everything he wrote in his bestselling book about the need for parental warmth and kindness, his own sons have said that he was a remote and chilly father himself and never kissed or cuddled them. And when, after his mentally ill and alcoholic first wife died, he married for a second time at the age of 73, he was apparently an equally unapproachable stepfather to the children of his new, 32-year-old wife.

So Spock was hardly a good role model, however good the advice he gave to the rest of the world sounds. Knowing how he behaved towards his own children, can his advice be considered more trustworthy than any other advice you might trip over elsewhere? Or, indeed, more trustworthy than the advice you might get from someone you already know whose children have demonstrably turned out fine?

Sloth help rules okay?

Sloths learn from their immediate world. As we have seen, the three-toed sloth is not well informed about the outside world, and doesn't really need to be.

The sloth doesn't try to tell us what to do – but we can learn by watching it.

The sloth is a great role model. We can see that in any number of ways it is at one with its world. And it certainly knows how to relax.

SELF HELP – WHO NEEDS THE HELP?

Dr Benjamin Spock isn't the only self-help guru whose personal credentials might make us question whether or not he was in the right business. There are others who might equally seem to be rather badly equipped for dishing out advice to the rest of the world. Here are a few examples.

- Would you take advice from the feminist relationship counsellor, Suzie Orbach, who gave advice to Princess Diana on the state of her marriage but declared publicly she would be unable to deal with a male client? Wouldn't it be rather useful to have some insight into a man's perspective if you are dealing with a marriage?

- Dr Laura Schlessinger, the American agony aunt, advised 12 million listeners on how to become good, old-fashioned, happy families, with mothers who stayed at home and found satisfaction in raising children, and fathers who brought home the bacon (or chicken, she's Jewish), but she built up a business empire of her own and married a divorced man. When Dr Laura's mother died, the body lay undiscovered for four months, and when it was discovered, Dr Laura blandly remarked that her mother had had no friends or close neighbours, so no-one had noticed – how sad.

- The father of psychotherapy, Carl Gustave Jung, thought he had two mothers, lived up a tower in the middle of a lake and used the excuse of his internalised female 'anima' to have affairs. Nevertheless, he became guru to half the Western world and inspired just about every psychometric test you've ever taken.

- Steve Andreas, the Neuro Linguistic Programming guru, wrote a book on achieving personal authenticity called *Transforming Yourself – Becoming Who You Want to Be* (which has been described like this: 'In this beautiful and brilliant book Steve Andreas addresses the core distinction of personal identity,' Stephen Gilligan PhD, author of *Therapeutic Trances* and *The Courage to Love*). Well, Steve would know what he's talking about when it comes to change and identity, having formerly been known as John O Stevens, but what about authenticity?

The problem with the self-help movement that seems to have taken over the world is that it's hard to tell who's in greater need of help, the gurus or the millions of people who buy their books.

Certainly, someone is making a lot of money out of the self-help industry. In 2004, self-help book sales in the UK alone totalled £39 million. Perhaps I am being overly cynical, but, given this figure, it's hardly in the interests of the writers of these books actually to achieve any improvements for their readership, is it? Perhaps that's why someone has chosen to write a book on leadership that takes as its model Sir Ernest Shackleton, who famously *didn't* make it to the South Pole. With an apparently straight face, the blurb even quotes the following: 'This book would have been required reading for my flight directors and mission controllers', from a certain Gene Koran, former flight director NASA, and the author of *Failure Is Not an Option*.

Wouldn't it make more sense to write a book on leadership that took Napoleon, Stalin or Hitler as a role model?

But what makes most sense to the self-help industry is to do a Chippendale on our everyday human problems, turning them into one-size-fits-all pathologies that have production-line solutions. That way you can keep up demand for the product and speed up growth, as well as, of course, profits.

Pathologise the problem

There's very little that you can't pathologise and therefore set up a demand for solutions to. One of the best and the brightest subjects for pathologising is childhood itself – this apparently is a trauma in its own right, according to one Alice Miller, a radical psychoanalyst. Even Benjamin Spock seems cuddly by comparison with her. She manages, in a string of books, among them the melodramatically entitled *The Drama of Being a Child*, to turn such horrors as a child being taught to say 'Please may I have some more?' into a cause of lifelong repression. Not since Dickens has so simple a request been transformed into such a successful money-spinner.

And once childhood has been pathologised, there are still:

- Relationships
- Weight
- Thinking style

- Emotional style
- Social behaviour
- Business behaviour
- Friendship
- Success
- Gender
- Mood

These areas are ripe for pathologising because we are all so detached from what might in the past have made us feel secure. These days, we are ready and willing to be told just how much of a mess and a failure we are, simply so that someone can fix us.

And when they've finished pathologising every possible aspect of our more vulnerable selves and made us feel so insecure that we are slavishly dependent on their advice, the self-help experts have another, alternative, approach up their sleeve: that is to persuade us that they, personally, have the ability to turn us, personally, into a powerful new kind of wonder-being – *Frogs Into Princes*, *Women Who Run with the Wolves*, *The Hero Within*, *Iron John*, *Awaken the Giant Within* ... that kind of mythic creature.

Is it me?

So now we've eaten our Chicken Soup for the Soul, Chatted with God, Looked after Our Emotions, Mapped Our Minds and Healed Our Hurt, meaning that now I'm Okay and You Are Okay, what next?

Isn't it bad enough that we believe we should dovetail into a total stranger's grand design for all our fixtures and fittings? But, even worse, we assume that we should aspire to fit their grand design for our hopes and aspirations too – even if a book called something like *How to Become More God-like* is far more likely to inspire fear and depression than energy and commitment in most of the people I know. Unless, of course, the reader has already been professionally trained in the, 'I, Myself and Me' language of ENHANCING SELF-ESTEEM, in which trillings of 'I'm so special' and 'Because I'm worth it' become commonplace, and godliness is probably the next logical stage of development.

You genuinely would have to be a believer in cosmic powers to fall for the notion that it's possible for any individual to have everything they want – either that or you'd have to fall for the astrology of a Mr Aly, who advertises his abilities on his fliers thus:

Specialist in all affective problems
Return immediately and definitely the person you love
Fidelity between husband and wife
Happiness, marriage problems
Relief from being bewitched, protection against all dangers
Making business more successful
Luck, Money
Love and Sexual Power.
100 per cent Success Guaranteed
Talisman available. I will break curses and protect you, and destroy the powers of Witchcraft, Black Magic and Bad Luck.
Prosperity Guaranteed
All your problems can be solved if you call Mr Aly on …

Mr Aly's naive advertising probably seems absurd, but is it really spectacularly different from what the self-help gurus have on offer? Mr Aly just hasn't learnt how to package his services for the middle classes. Believing in what he offers is no more gullible than believing 'The Power of Your Subconscious Mind' when it tells you that the feeling of wealth will produce wealth in reality, or accepting one of the main principles of NLP, which is that, 'If one person can do something, anyone can learn to do it'. Well, perhaps not the eight-year-old struggling to play Mozart.

This self-help stuff is all really about re-inventing ourselves as somebody different and better – which rather begs the question of why we should feel inadequate in the first place. Are we somehow deficient as human beings, not walking on two legs or failing to put food into the right orifice, or something like that? Perhaps we should feel generally rather pleased to make it through a day walking, talking and thinking simultaneously; after all, we'd make television programs about a monkey that could do that. But it's much more in the interests of the motivational and inspirational self-improvement trainers, who re-invent themselves on an almost daily basis, to keep our insecurities alive and kicking. That way they can make bucket-loads of money training us to be more like them. But if we take our lead from the sloth instead and learn to accept ourselves as we find ourselves, we'll save ourselves an awful lot of trouble, not to mention money, and find life altogether more relaxing and fulfilling.

Just imagine if people like da Vinci, Shakespeare, Newton, Dickens and Turing had been counselled, therapied and sorted so they lived out their lives in blameless and harmonious normality – what would we have missed out on? If Dickens had integrated all the opposing elements of his personality we'd probably never have had Fagin or Miss Havisham, and if Turing had learnt the Seven Habits of Highly Effective People perhaps we'd never have had the computer.

IF IT AIN'T BROKE, DON'T FIX IT?

Self-help can only really be necessary if we aren't functioning properly in the first place, can't it? Which rather begs the question what functioning properly means. Which in turn begs the question what we are functioning for. Do you know the answer?

The sloth knows. The sloth knows that the business of a sloth's life is to be. And for sloths as a species to carry on being for a very long time.

We seem to have rather confused the business of our lives. It's no longer enough for us simply to be; we have started to expect much more than that, and by expecting far too much, we've ended up enjoying far too little.

If we weren't so busy trying to make life perfect, and then trying to make ourselves perfect to fit our perfect lives (advertising, you have a lot to answer for), we might have enough time left over to enjoy living the lives we actually have a bit more. The present situation reminds me of a play I once saw, starring Prunella Scales as a tense, perfectionist woman. She described an evening when she had organised her meal to absolute perfection. She had cooked it, tidying up the kitchen as she went, soaked the pots and pans, laid her tray beautifully, washed up the dishes, and taken herself off to bed. It was only when she was lying there that she remembered that the one thing she had overlooked in her perfectly organised evening was eating the supper she'd cooked.

We can have perfect *Home and Garden*-type houses, manicured lawns and immaculately organised and controlled lives, involving 'a good job', pilates and personal therapy, but there will still be an awful lot of people out there who'll wonder what's missing once they've achieved it all and gone home and made their evening meal. Having it all isn't having everything – otherwise why Pete Doherty?

WHY DO WE FEEL THAT NEED TO COMPETE?

Perhaps believing we are inadequate and feeling that we should be busier perfecting ourselves starts with the school swot:

> Haven't you finished that yet? I finished mine ages ago.

> Ooh, you shouldn't say that thing – Mrs Rowbotham said it wasn't nice!

> That was easy-peasy. Shall I do some more, Mrs Rowbotham?

And perhaps it's time we grew up and started to reclaim ourselves from the tyrannical need to compete with some of the most advanced life forms we come across, especially when we only come across them in the media. I mean, what percentage of humanity do they represent? Our chances of being as beautiful as Nicole Kidman or as successful as Alan Sugar must be infinitely lower than those of winning the Lottery. But still we keep on trying to emulate these kinds of people, even though we are more or less condemned to failure, however hard we try. Are we all masochists?

How many of us believe that we could copy Einstein's feats of intelligence? Or want to copy St Francis of Assisi's enormous self-denial (he wounded his hands and feet in imitation of Jesus's stigmata and asked pardon of his body, which he called Brother Ass, for the self-inflicted penances of vigils, fasts, flagellations and the use of a hair shirt)? Yet many of us still think we should be able to achieve class-swot levels of business brilliance, personal beauty, emotional functionality and positive thinking. Aiming so high, or trying to change so much about ourselves, can only result in disappointment 95 per cent of the time. That is, unless we are really persuaded that by buying a particular brand of lipstick we can suddenly morph into Kate Moss or by chanting a particular mantra we can suddenly discover the hidden (perhaps entombed?) business strength of Richard Branson.

People really don't change that much. Most of the spade work in life is done very young; after that the rest is mostly weeding. Fat people most often continue having to fight fat, short people always have to fight short, and addicts generally have to go on fighting one addiction or another (rehab has a surprisingly low success rate). Clever people don't stop being clever, and engineers don't suddenly become stupid at engineering, so why should stupid people start being clever, or insensitive men become emotionally literate?

The idea that we all have choices about all these things is simply exhausting, and the implication that we could somehow choose to become perfect if we weren't being indolent only makes it all the harder for us to put our hands up and say:

> Enough, no more. I'm just fine the way I am. I'm not a child molester, I can make it to the shops on my own and I know where to put my peas, so can I be considered a good enough person, please?

In fact it might be better, and much more entertaining, for us all if more of us didn't aim for perfection but for quirkiness instead. Jane Austen, who I suspect had quite a healthy inner sloth, made what she saw as the advantages of imperfection perfectly clear, writing in Pride and Prejudice:

> For what do we live, but to make sport for our neighbours, and laugh at them in our turn?

She certainly took advantage herself of all the fun to be had from recreating other people's imperfections on the page, and there's a lot to be said for getting our own enjoyment from being absurd, controversial, narrow-minded, eccentric or even plain dull.

ALLOW YOURSELF TO BE DULL

Yes, there's a lot to be said for dull, as the numbers of men flocking to sign up for the Dull Men's Club are discovering (on the internet, of course, you don't actually have to turn up). Here they can look up articles on matters as dull as park benches, everything anyone ever wanted to know about concrete, the pylon of the month or (and I'm afraid there's no way this can be dull) the fabulous shoelace site. The club was set up by men who decided they'd had enough of being expected to be perfect, exciting, smart, or anything very much, and that they'd just like to be quietly at one with their very own dull imperfections.

Actually, after the tedium of self-help, it sounds quite exciting.

But allowing oneself to be dull, having the balls to stand out from the crowd of over-achievers, busy, busy, busy perfect mothers, knock-kneed catwalk model clones and adrenalin junkies, does entail a sort of heroism. Those of us who are prepared to stand up and defend our right to be dull, are also saying that we are prepared to think and live for ourselves. And, presumably, that will include thinking negatively if we want, and ageing as and when nature takes its course.

It's hard to imagine a dull man trying to 'hold back the years' or thinking that perhaps he should move with his cheese (as business guru Dr Spencer Johnson suggests in his bestselling book *Who Moved My Cheese?*), which surely makes him even more heroic. A cardigan and a facelift? Slippers and a one-minute mind makeover? No, dull men hold out against these kinds of tyrannies, which must put them up there among freedom-fighters everywhere.

Would that we could all say we are prepared to stand by our inner sloth, embrace our true nature and reject the idea that Joan Rivers looks younger than her years or that humans have survived as long as they have by saying things like, 'It is safer to search in the maze than remain in a cheeseless situation' (I refer to Dr Spencer Johnson again). But, sadly, most of us do allow ourselves to be fooled most of the time. We allow programmes like *Ten Years Younger* to raise the age game (if not the allowable age) for everyone and are persuaded that we can and should change ourselves. Perhaps one day we'll look back at a time when we were told to 'act your age' and think nostalgically about the lost possibility of growing up to wear comfortable clothes, drink tea in the afternoon, and care more about what we are experiencing in life than about how other people are experiencing us.

Relentless optimism

But while having to look too young for our age is a personal trial, having to think too cheerily for reality often turns out to be a public one. We all know how immensely irritating it is to hear someone say, as we are innocently walking down the street, 'Cheer up, it may never happen' – especially when 'it' already has. But imagine how you would feel if the irritatingly positive thinker were your doctor, newly tutored in the art of positive psychology:

> Well, let's look on the bright side and assume it is not cancer. We won't bother with a scan.

How ghastly would that be?

And yet that's how relentless optimists want us to be. We should all think positively all of the time, and then the world will become perfect and we'll all (each of us individually of course) have everything we could possibly want. But miserabilists everywhere recently received a positive shot in the arm when American Professor of Psychology, David Dunning, who was researching optimism and pessimism, was reported as having discovered that high levels of confidence were actually linked to high levels of incompetence and that in fact pessimists prepare better for risk. Well, what do you know? To a sloth these findings would make intuitive sense – when you see a sabre-toothed tiger, don't hope for the best, run.

NOT PERFECT YET, AND NOT LOOKING TO BE, THANK YOU VERY MUCH

If we think back to the prisoners on page 9, we will recall that their hopes and ambitions were fairly modest, and pretty much focused on the local and domestic. I'm not going to argue that prisoners have acquired some kind of mystical wholeness in prison – far from it! I am going to say that at some stage they have, fairly obviously, expected just a wee bit more out of life than was realistic, and so have had to learn the hard way about disappointment and limiting the scope of one's ambitions. Perhaps that acceptance of limitations will last for some of them, perhaps not, but at least in the short term it has meant that they have also learnt to appreciate the fact that the greatest pleasures they've had in their lives came out of living fully in the moment.

Living fully in the moment, once we've stopped expecting too much perfection either from ourselves or from life, can be full of delights. Take the story of Sergeant Major William (Bill) Brown and his family for example.

They were all invited to a rather grand family wedding, husband, wife, and three kids: Sally 15, Wayne eight, and Tommy five. Bill wanted to impress family members he hadn't seen for ages who would be at the wedding, and as he prided himself on his organisational skills, he made sure all was as it should be. He filled his two-year-old, regularly serviced, reliable car with petrol, air, oil and water. He washed it and polished it and made sure it did him proud, and with each family member in their best bib and tucker they all set off for the wedding in *very* good time. There were only 100 kilometres to go and they had two and a half hours in hand.

Sixty kilometres into the journey, and half-way into a remote valley, the car broke down. Bill Brown was far too organised and sensible not to have breakdown insurance and his mobile phone with him, fully charged, so though he was furious about the car, he didn't foresee any real problems. There was still plenty of time. Only the car was in a valley, and the phone had no reception so, getting crosser by the minute, he set off to find a place where the phone would work. It was the best part of a kilometre away, and then when he got through to the breakdown organisation he was told that they were very sorry but, because of a big accident, all vehicles were busy and he might have to wait as long as an hour for one to get to him.

Bill Brown was so used to organising things to perfection, and he had been so looking forward to getting to the wedding on time and showing his family off, and he was so stressed by everything he couldn't control, that he was unable to see that the valley he stomped back down was one of the most beautiful places in the land.

The breakdown truck came early and they did get to the wedding on time, but it was already too late for Bill.

Twenty years on, Major and Mrs Brown and Sally remember cousin Emily's wedding day as that awful time the car broke down and they nearly didn't make it to the wedding. Wayne remembers cousin Emily's wedding day as the time he had to get all dressed up and Dad was cross all day, but Tommy has a lovely memory of some time when they all stopped in a wonderful place by a stream and he watched the tadpoles in their millions. Same day, different moments.

Why do so many of us lose the ability to be in the moment like that? It's no good saying because we need to get things done, make progress, or take responsibility. There was nothing more that Bill Brown could have done that day after he'd made the phone call, but he kept himself high on frustration. He felt he was falling short of his own high standards of competence, and he kept imagining an embarrassing scene in which his family turned up late at the wedding, and made themselves look silly in front of all the posh guests. But it wasn't a war situation and he had his expectations of himself all mixed up. Once he'd done everything possible by phoning for help he could easily have afforded to be more sloth-like; it would have cost him nothing at all. If he hadn't felt he had so much to live up to, he could have enjoyed spending time watching the tadpoles with Tommy. How many of us can honestly say that we haven't lost a thousand similar opportunities to enjoy the best of what's around us, and at the same time to store up memories of some of the purest kinds of pleasure?

The person who asked of the woman walking down the street in her curlers, 'Where could she be going that's so much more important than where she is now?' must have felt that the future can never be special enough to make us forget ourselves in the present. And she (it would have to have been a woman, wouldn't it?) would also probably have been a true believer in Robbie Burns's lines:

> The best laid schemes o' mice an' men
> Gang aft agley.

Unlike the woman in the street. How annoying for her to have been knocked down by a bus while she was in full preparation for her big night out – she would have had to have been buried in her curlers.

Which, in a roundabout way, leads us back to the start of the book. If we want to be able to get more value out of life, in the way that Tommy got more value out of the wedding trip and had better memories to look back on than the rest of his family, then we need to be more aware of the moment we are living in, and of the value we might be getting out of it, than we so often are in our future perfect culture.

SLOTH HELP

Self-help; self-improvement; positive thinking; body, mind and image makeovers ... they are all about how rubbish we must be at the moment. That means we are broke in some way and need fixing – *their* kind of fixing, be they 'experts', media stars or self-help gurus.

Well, hopefully there are enough people out there objecting to being told they are broke that right now I am knocking at an open door and we can all insist in a rising crescendo,

> I don't need fixing, thank you very much!

And so you might, quite reasonably, be thinking, what's this sloth help all about? Well, it is not about fixing you. At the beginning of the book, we talked about how the world seems to be spinning faster than we can keep up with, how it expects us to be on the go 24/7 – shopping at midnight, doing press-ups at dawn, working through lunch – just so we can build *a better future*, not to mention a better version of ourselves. This book is saying let's have a better present, and you don't have to train yourself up to achieve that. You don't have to fix yourself at all. If anything needs fixing, it's the world, not us. But, hey, let the world look after itself for five minutes. It's not going anywhere.

So we don't need self-help, but we do need *sloth help*, because we're a little out of practice at doing what comes naturally and it's good to watch a professional.

Note that: a professional, not an expert. Sloths aren't like some of the high-profile relationship counsellors, psychoanalysts, therapists, gurus and agony aunts, who go to *enormous* lengths to hide the reality of their lives from their clients and from the world. With the sloth it's rarely a case of 'do as I say, not as I do'.

The sloth is well practised and would practise what it preaches if it preached at all, but preaching is not quite its style – that's too much like hard work. With the sloth what you see is what you get: a creature born and bred to take the strain out of living, one that doesn't have to keep learning new tricks or improving on the past when the past still works perfectly well.

What the sloth learns at its mother's knees will generally stand the species in good stead for another million years or so – that's so refreshing, isn't it? Just think, no need for teenage rebellion, for going out 'looking like that' (so cold!), or for any of those pimply embraces with the kids from the wrong side of town. For a youthful sloth there is simply the leisurely acceptance that nothing changes, the family heirlooms don't have to be chucked out, the crest can stay on the china, and the family sayings hold true – you've no duty to disprove any of the following sloth-like maxims:

- Waste not, want not.
- Hunger never saw bad bread.
- Slow and steady wins the race.
- One today is worth two tomorrows.
- Good things come in small packages.
- Neither a borrower nor a lender be.
- Beauty is in the eye of the beholder.
- A bird in the hand is worth two in the bush.
- Discretion is the better part of valour.
- Enough is as good as a feast.
- You are what you eat.

Which must be bliss. For the baby sloth those old saws are as good a set of beliefs to live by as any they may ever come across, so they don't have to go off in search of something new and challenging. No, they save themselves the trouble and expend their energy in hanging around in a leafy hammock instead.

Imagine if we too could assume that what worked for our families in the past would still work for us today – that we didn't have to learn whole new ways of being from a thousand different external 'expert' sources, and then make decisions about what was likely to work best for us. How are we supposed to know?

We could (and do) spend great chunks of our lives these days working out just what the best solutions to the problems of our lives might be. Would it really make a great deal of difference (apart from to the quality of our lives) if we worked instead on the assumption that nothing's perfect and that what worked well enough for our parents and grandparents would probably work just as well for us?

Now I'm not being utterly simple-minded. I'm not suggesting that we turn the clock back to 1520 so we can spend our lives up to the neck in rustic mire or to 1850, when we might just have found ourselves working alongside the pit ponies in deep Victorian mines. And neither am I suggesting that it would be a great idea to take your cue from your family if your family has largely been composed of mass murderers, hermits or depressives. But I *am* saying that we spend too long re-inventing the wheel, throwing the baby out with the bathwater, fixing things that aren't broken, etc. and that this is time we could spend accumulating 'pleasure treasure'. If our short lifetime is all we have on earth, why spend it relearning that Men are From Mars and Women from Venus, when our grandmothers never doubted it? Or that it's no fun getting up at the crack of dawn in all weathers to trudge long distances to work and then come home to do all the housework and cooking? Or that, in the long term 'I want, never gets'? Or that Milton was right, back in 1634, when he wrote in *Comus*:

> Do not charge most innocent Nature,
> As if she would her children should be riotous
> With her abundance. She, good cateress,
> Means her provision only to the good,
> That live according to her sober laws
> And holy dictate of spare Temperance.
> If every just man that now pines with want
> Had but a moderate and beseeming share
> Of that which lewdly-pamper'd Luxury
> Now heaps upon some few with vast excess,
> Nature's full blessings would be well dispens'd
> In unsuperfluous even proportion,
> And she no whit encumber'd with her store;
> And then the giver would be better thank'd,

His praise due paid; for swinish gluttony
Ne'er looks to Heav'n amidst his gorgeous feast,
But with besotted base ingratitude
Crams, and blasphemes his feeder.

The language of his poem may be a little different from today's, but its ideas come straight from the green heart of every modern major political party. We also hear them from the folk at Oxfam and from TV programmes like *You Are What You Eat*.

The truth of this wisdom was known only too well by our grandparents. Why would they have gone to such great lengths to make life less laborious if they found doing the work of three people stimulating and fun? Why would they have told their kids to eat their greens if they hadn't learnt the hard way what was good for them? Why did they subscribe to a philosophy of 'waste not want not' if they didn't know all too well that food doesn't always grow on trees? Why did they send boisterous little boys outside to use up their energy in competitive games if they'd noticed that exercise made them aggressive? These were people who knew because they'd been there and done it. Why did we stop listening to them?

I'm afraid we're back to the so-called experts again. They are the ones who detached us from our lived experience. Or to put it another way, they are the ones who told us:

We know more than we think you do.

And then they gave us a whole lot of work to do. Thanks a bunch.

We need to get back in touch with practices and solutions that can be seen to have worked in the past – practices and solutions centred on reducing excess, sourcing products locally and taking more pleasure in what we already have.

We also need to learn to accept ourselves more. The sloth doesn't see itself as a problem, so unlike us it's not buzzing about like a f---t in a bucket trying to put itself right all the time. The big gain from that is that the sloth can live in an unhurried and measured way, one that allows it to get all the necessaries done without neglecting itself, starving, doing other creatures down, or using up all the world's resources, but leaving itself plenty of time simply to be.

The sloth is at peace, not at war, with itself, and the brilliant thing is that what we can learn from it is a lot more authentic than what we can learn from issue-driven experts, or from glossy magazines, or TV programmes, because we can see the evidence of its success right in front of us.

The sloth is a very relaxed being. If we follow some of its principles, we can learn to be very relaxed beings too.

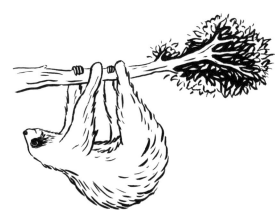

5

Sloth helplines

Relationships, sex, shopping, cars – the sloth can help us sort out our attitudes to all of these modern phenomena.

Now you really *know* I'm barking, whereas before you might only have suspected it! No, of course sloths aren't intimate with these matters themselves. They don't spice up their sluggish lives by reading saucy magazines in bed or trawl the Bluewater mall for the latest in green fashion (though you'd be amazed at some of the places they do pop up). This is a very serious book; it's not into all that anthropomorphic fantasy stuff at all. Do away immediately with any images you might have conjured up of seductive sloths à la Jessica Rabbit, in satin and heels, or of webwise sloths snapping up designer bargains on Amazon.com, and come back down to the very earthy reality of the genuine article, to the reality of the sloth itself. Because that's quite fascinating enough in its own right without needing to be 'tooned' up.

Of course, the sloth is supremely fascinating to us in ways that only that great TV wildlife presenter David Attenborough could truly bring to life, as he breathily takes us crunching and cracking our way deep into the steamy central American rainforest, sweeping us high up into the canopy where the shaggy leaf-mould form of the sloth dangles sleepily among the branches. But it is also a little bit fascinating to us because of what can only be described as its amazingly chilled attitude to life. Okay, so that's anthropomorphising it too in a way, but it's difficult to convey the intention of the book without anthropomorphising just a bit. Perhaps it would be more scrupulous to say we can learn to adapt our current attitudes by looking at the way sloths live their lives, but it's rather easier to understand how if we assume that sloths have attitudes themselves.

⚡ Sloth helplines

The bottom line is that looking at the sloth's way of living genuinely can help to kickstart the process of questioning our previously unchallenged dedication to speed and growth, because sloths show us that speed and growth are not absolutely built into nature but that life can unfold happily without all kinds of ra-ra going off like fizz-bombs in the bath. And once we have started to question this allegiance, we can allow ourselves to begin to consider various ways in which we might be able to bring a more relaxed attitude to the business of life ourselves – even to the apparently unlikely kinds of business mentioned at the head of this chapter: relationships, sex, shopping and cars.

But before we go on to look at the innumerable areas of life in which the sloth can teach us a thing or two, let's remind ourselves of some of the innumerable attributes of the sloth that we looked at in Chapter 3:

- ⚡ Sloths are adaptable.
- ⚡ Sloths don't get unnecessarily stressed or waste their energy.
- ⚡ Sloths don't obsess about grooming.
- ⚡ Sloths don't overstimulate themselves with additives or activity, and they sleep very well.
- ⚡ Sloths are very flexible.
- ⚡ Sloths are not fussy about food and source it locally.
- ⚡ Sloths are into natural disposal of waste.
- ⚡ Sloths don't compete with one another.
- ⚡ Sloths aren't showy.
- ⚡ Sloths have thick skins.
- ⚡ Sloths don't over-protect their young.
- ⚡ Sloths rely on themselves and their closest group members for support.
- ⚡ Sloths are (or appear to be) quite remarkably contented.
- ⚡ Sloths simply are what they are and don't keep re-inventing and rearranging themselves.

These are the characteristics that work well for the sloth; they are also a pretty useful reference point for what works well for people – which is why I'm restating them here.

Having got that reminder down, we can now go on to look at the multitude of things, beginning with those mentioned at the start of this chapter, that we hone in on as targets in our never-ending quest to make our lives more perfect and keep the change ball rolling. They are all, in one way or another, connected with our need to change some aspect of ourselves, and each one represents a part of us that an 'expert' or 'authority' has said suffers from some kind of design fault and really, really could be improved upon – with their expert and helpful input, of course.

Now, lest it should be said that I, too, am jumping on that bandwagon, I should like to issue a disclaimer. I don't think there are such design faults, so I'm not trying to fix them; I'm simply aiming to strip away the most recent, and pointless, fixings imposed by others. I think it is time we got back down to our more authentic, pre-reformation, selves. And anyway, it was the sloth that did it – I'm just acting as the sloth's intermediary, the representative, the voice. The sloth has far, far better things to do than try to meddle in someone else's life.

So we will leave the sloth, perhaps doing its coconut impression, swinging gently in the breeze, as we poor busy humans, trek out in search of subjects over which the sloth can cast its mildly appraising eye. When our worries over some of the most pressing of them are put to the sloth, its wise thoughts, developed and matured over thousands of years, thoughts that have seen other species come and go, will be delivered, of course, by proxy.

SLOTH HELPLINE NUMBER ONE – RELATIONSHIPS AND SEX

Phew, what a place to start! On the other hand, the sloth is not too squeamish about these things and is able to take the plunge fearlessly when absolutely necessary.

More than 80 per cent of us say that our close relationships are the most important thing in our lives. We'll take a look at friendship later; here we're concerned with sexual and love relationships and the effect that they have on us.

Well, clearly they affect our emotions, and emotions being what they are, that means that our relationships affect most areas of our lives, including work – as any fool knows who has ever worked in a confined space with someone whose romance is in a critical state! So our working life and probably all-round workplace relationships are affected by the state of our intimate relationships, and quadruply so if our intimate relationship is with a work colleague.

The state of our emotions has a huge impact on our psychological state, too, so it's unsurprising that good and stable long-term relationships make for less depression and better overall mental health. In fact, in a US survey of 10,000 people, those who remained married to their first long-term partner were seen to have much stronger psychological health and a *much higher life expectancy* than those whose first long-term relationship had split up. People who'd never been in a relationship in the first place were also healthier, mentally and physically, than those who had split up, but nothing like as healthy as the ones who stayed the course. Co-habiting relationships, the first choice for many, are better for us than being single, in terms of health, happiness, stability and the cost of hotel rooms, but statistically they don't offer the same advantages as marriage. So marriage, that longest-standing gold standard of relationship, seems to be of benefit to us.

Bizarre, then, that we seem to be making such a hash of it. The divorce rate in both the US and the UK is currently approaching an all-time high, with 155,000 divorces in 2005 in England and Wales (compared with 141,000 in the mid-nineties). The most recent UK statistic for marriages is 267,700 in 2003 (virtually an all-time low) of which only 158,560 were first-time marriages.

There are other benefits of long-term marriage, too. Researchers from the US, who have been tracking couples since 1979, claim that when people divorce they lose three-quarters of their net financial worth, and that makes them poorer than singletons who've never been married, who in their turn are still worth only half what married people are. Not only would the research seem to prove that two really can live as cheaply as one, it also rather challenges the glitzy TV stereotype of the designer-clad single who leads the life of Riley while their sad married cousin munches on beans on toast in a charity frock.

Marriage is the best relationship of all for our health and our wealth, but we are just not that into it. Do we really want to be ill and poor? Do we really want the worst possible relationship situation, while at the same time believing that good relationships are the most important thing in the world to us? Where's the logic in any of it?

Perhaps, once again, the answer lies in our grimly narrow focus on the terrible twins of speed and perfectibility, and our timid dependency on other people (especially experts and expert commentators) to tell us how we should redesign our lives to be more up to the minute – how we need to fix what ain't necessarily broken.

What television has to answer for

One of the reasons why TV has an awful lot to answer when it comes to our crazy relationship with relationships is that it spreads the word from the life design gods more quickly than any other medium. TV is also responsible for exposing us to all that is good and bad (and terrible!) in social trends. Where our grandparents had to wait weeks or even months to discover, by word of mouth or newsprint, what was happening lifestyle-wise in the world beyond their village, now we see it happening on television even more quickly than it happens in reality. Which of course makes us think we are getting left behind.

Take the fashion for instant romance. Just how long does it take someone to fall 'in love' on soap operas such as *Coronation Street* and *Neighbours*? And it's never anything less than The Big One, is it? No self-respecting character in a soap ever thinks that perhaps they are having a bit of a crush on someone or that Sharon is a good reliable sort and they could probably see their way to falling a little bit in love with her, given time. No, the ratings war (just another name for the profit principle) makes sure that the love game in soaps gets faster and faster, until it ends up like a mad version of Wimbledon, with people diving after balls all over the show. And, of course, what we see on television must represent reality ... otherwise why would people send flowers of condolence when some soap character dies?

But almost as soon as our soap star has hit upon their 'soul mate', their absolutely perfect other, the one to whom they pledge their teary-eyed all (preferably in a quivering voice and a Chardonnay gown), they immediately, with scarcely a fag paper in between, get down to the gritty business of telling them in how many ways they are a wipe-out in comparison with somebody else, who just happens 'to really, really understand me, and my needs, better than any one I've ever met. But I really, really never meant to hurt you.'

And that's one of the other factors in the equation: the belief that we are here to seek out perfection in relationships and should be able to have as many goes as it's going to take to find it, while having 'the right' to hurt anyone who gets in the way – although, of course, we 'never set out to hurt them'. Really?

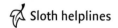

It's those experts again

Yes, TV may well have a lot to answer for, but it's not the only reason that our relationships are more stressful than is good for our health. TV may take our desire for entertainment more seriously than it takes our well-being, but we can hardly lay all the blame for our relationship problems on a box in the corner of the sitting room (and bedroom, and kitchen and kids' rooms). There are also our old friends the 'experts'.

Things are on the turn a bit now, but for years the relationship experts favoured challenge and change; the status quo simply had to go. Any letter to an agony aunt suggesting that a relationship was getting stale would be answered with the instruction to 'leave if it's not working for you'. Therapists and counsellors have intoned 'better out than in' until we've been brainwashed into believing that honesty in relationships is more desirable than kindness. The zeitgeist articles and books that have poured from sex sages' pens have left none of us in any doubt that living together is just as good as marriage (if not infinitely better, because clearly less restricting, more chic and cosmopolitan), that anyone questioning that self-evident truth is moribund and judgemental and that marriage is probably no more than legalised prostitution anyway. Experimentation was the religion of the day for trendy therapists.

There wasn't a whisker of evidence for most of it, but who cared? This was a whole new world. Gone was the oh so damaging past of emotional and sexual repression, marital slavery and, dear god, convention. Out with the old, in with the new, winds of change, fresh fields, pastures new. Utterly exhausting.

Sex post-1963

But not half as exhausting as the sexual revolution itself.

Had nobody ever had sex before Larkin's 1963? It's a serious question, serious enough to require a more scholarly debate than a sloth would engage in, so we'll just give you Sussex University's prospectus details on their course 1963: Sexual Revolution in Britain:

> According to the poet Philip Larkin, sexual intercourse 'began' in 1963; the 'swinging sixties' have certainly been characterised as a decade when sexual relationships were subject to fundamental change. Taking 1963 as its starting point, this course will examine the shifting nature of sexual and emotional intimacy across 20th-century Britain. Is it accurate to characterise certain decades as periods of sexual revolution

and others as periods of sexual conservatism? If so, how do we account for this kind of historical change? The course will pay close attention to longer-term demographic shifts and attempt to account for the rising popularity of marriage until the late 1960s and its declining popularity from the 1970s. Along the way we will examine the social implications of birth control availability, the significance of historically specific shifts in the age at first marriage, courtship etiquette, changing sexual practices and cultural constructions of 'love'.

The sloth's life is not a busy one, so we'll leave Sussex University to take the strain on that one.

Anyway, whatever happened before 1963, ever since then we've been taught to expect even more than what might be considered our fair share of sex from every possible source, and good sex too, none of your 'wham, bam, thank you ma'am', as our given right. Sex is no longer just what happens in marriage, or just what gets done to unwilling girls by moustachioed men. Sex has become part of the Gender Game – and so part of the Equality Game – an aspect of the Lifestyle Olympics, with everyone expected to compete for medals.

Tap the words 'sex sites' into Google and you'll find 145 million sites ready to cater for any taste you may currently have, so there's no need to be, and absolutely no excuse for being, less than perfectly up to speed in your sport of choice.

Long gone is the time when sex shops hid themselves shamefacedly down alleys, and the pop-up *Kama Sutra* was the most exotic thing you were likely to find in any one of them outside Soho. Nowadays, if we're feeling peckish at lunch time we can nip totally unashamedly into a high street chain of sex shops and pick up edible candy knickers and thongs in a range of styles and flavours to munch on. If we're feeling inclusively inclined we can choose to dress ourselves up as Ivana and Boris, or Mustafa (I'll leave the rest to your imagination) and Meera in the name of multi-cultural fantasy. If we're feeling, like, really liberated we can have fun with a Rampant Rabbit Thruster while dressed as a harlot/cyber doll in chains or carry out the thrusting enjoyably trussed up as a slave. But it will always bring a cosy nostalgic glow to know that comedy posing pouches are standing up well and there's still a Naughty Nurse on night duty.

The tremendous success of *Bridget Jones's Diary* is partly down to Helen Fielding's comic skill in sending up the sexual schizophrenia that has resulted from the confusion of gender politics and sexual liberation.

Shouldn't a girl have the right to dress in big pants if they're comfy – but what if the guy finds out? Then again, should a girl care, because why should she be dependent on a man? But then again, isn't a hero written by a spinster several hundred years ago more interesting than a modern man who, after all, is still only after one thing, and a girl doesn't need that, does she? She can look after herself, can't she? But what are those Alsatians doing there? And why is a girl dressing up in old-fashioned male fantasy clothes not left alone when it's perfectly clear that it's only a post-modern ironic nod to the past, and she can be in charge of her own sexuality, can't she? But why doesn't he fancy her?

Sex and romance have always been two sides of the same coin, but nowadays sex is the common currency, and for some people that has made it a tyranny. How does a girl say no if that makes her look like a sad sap, and how does a guy get away with not trying it on from the start without looking like a complete wuss? It's just expected that virtually any male and female combo (and pretty much every other combo too) will be 'up for it'. Sex has now become the rightful goal of any two people who just happen to meet up under any circumstances.

Obviously it's the rightful goal in a good, intimate relationship. Which means that relationships that don't have enough high-quality sex in them are seen as failing relationships, however good other parts of them might be. And that goes for many marriages, as those of us who read the 'Help!' letters in magazines (and no, I don't believe you don't) know only too well. Marriages nowadays are routinely expected to be as romantic and busily sexual after umpteen years as any first date in a soap opera. Think of the numbers of adverts that coyly play with the idea of some glamorous couple acting out steamy romps in hidden corners in order to hide their 'illicit' fun from their own cutesy little moppets. Once upon a time, wives in adverts used to be all Oxo Katy feeding a man's hunger; now they're all Sexy Sadie feeding a man's fantasy. None of which makes it any easier on those of us who, while perfectly happy to frolic along with the best, would also quite like not to be forced to define our success in the marital stakes by bed alone.

Or, in fact, by the standards set in any other perfect fantasy. What the truly sloth-like soul would prefer to define success by is how at peace with ourselves it leaves us feeling. Which is pretty close to where we came in at the start of this chapter: close relationships that work well make us feel good.

Living together

In the popular view, living together is a more up-to-the-minute alternative to marriage. It's generally seen as freer and more flexible, suggesting that we should be able to feel more relaxed within it than we ever could within the restrictions of marriage. So is living together better for us – better, that is, in terms of enjoyment and feeling at peace with ourselves?

Now the sloth is perfectly indifferent to questions of morality (having none to speak of itself), but it would have to take a serious look at statistics suggesting that while a co-habiting relationship may at first feel every bit as emotionally committed as a married one, it has a less than 4 per cent chance of lasting out ten years, compared with 80 per cent for a marriage – not the most stabilising and peaceful of prospects. Also, the majority of co-habitees, who don't happen to be living in sin with a pop star, will find considerably less money around than in a marriage. In addition to which, a partner in a co-habiting set-up is more likely to be depressed than a single person who's never shacked up in the first place (perhaps, in the case of mixed-sex couples who have children, because the woman is more likely to end up as a single self-supporting parent, and the man as a father who can't get access to his kids).

You can only conclude that a sloth would not recommend it.

Are friends relations?

Where marriage left off in the popularity stakes, friendship seems to have taken over. Many people under 40 will now say their friends mean at least as much, if not more, than their family. 'You can choose your friends' etc. And let's face it, there are always some family members we wouldn't choose. In fact there are some family members we wouldn't wish even on our worst enemies, but we are rather stuck with them.

And that's one of the beauties of friendship: we don't have to be stuck with it. So, in our age of impermanence and hurry, it has pretty obvious attractions. On the other hand, if the success of television programmes like *Sex and the City* and *Friends* are anything to go by, friendships are usually seen as outlasting, and certainly outperforming, other relationships by a mile. Having a grotty day? Well, that generally includes some formulaic variant on bad hair, bad luck and bad erotic or romantic encounter, and is nothing that a latte or cocktail with friends can't put right.

It's really quite interesting that one of the original 'life can be lonely in the city, but friends can make everything better' American soaps, *Cheers*, threw a bunch of rather sad, and totally deluded losers together in a not very upmarket bar. Failure, and especially failure in love, was the choppy sea that they swam in, and friendship was the life raft they knew they could always just about cling to. But only until they reached the dry land of success – which everyone but they knew was never going to happen. And that was one of the biggest jokes of all.

How different from *Sex and the City* and *Friends*, in which friendship is the sea the protagonists swim in, and they are loving it. Whatever happens to any of the characters – love, success, failure – it's all made better, or even better still, by friendships, their primary relationships. They outlast financial crises, illness, envy, jealousy, love, babies, sterility, parents, siblings, migration, promotions and demotions, love, and even the intervention into the friendship of sex itself. This is especially true in *Friends*, in which even when characters have sexual relationships with one another, they still define themselves as friends first and foremost.

Which is presumably what Sarah Ferguson was going on about when she called Prince Andrew her 'bestest friend'. Sex and marriage can come and go, but friendship lives on, ever present in your life, ever ready to come to your aid in a crisis. This seems to be the message of the moment.

The propaganda may all be a bit exaggerated, and it may be that people (as ever) are more inclined to believe the glossy hype on the TV screen than the more mutable reality in front of their noses – who do you actually see at Christmas, your coiffed and wise-cracking friends or your mum, dad and little brother? – but friendship has come on a bit since *Hancock's Half Hour*, and most of us do get a lot of fun and pleasure from spending time with our mates. After all, they are the ones least likely to have high expectations of us, most likely to accept our imperfections and happiest simply to hang around with us.

In other words, they are the ones most likely to recognise our inner sloth.

Dear Sloth

These would not be credible helplines if we weren't prepared to respond directly to people's genuine confusion in the face of life's current complications and perplexities. So the sloth, very sportingly, has offered to volunteer its own experience and to make a few suggestions to those optioned out souls as to what, over thousands of years, it has found most effective in achieving the level of almost complete quietude and chill it has always enjoyed.

A small disclaimer: since it has been important to maintain the sloth's calm detachment, a certain amount of intervention, interpretation and ghost-writing must be understood in the material that follows.

Dear Sloth

I don't know what to do and I need your help. I've been married for ten years to a lovely man, but the problem is I just don't love him any more. And now there's somebody else on the scene and I think I'm falling in love with him.

Ever since I can remember, I have wanted to be around people in the music business or films. It all looked so much more exciting than the kind of life my parents had – although they were very contented together, their lives were quite ordinary. And then I met my husband at a party. He was in a band, one I'd seen on TV, so I couldn't believe my luck. He was good-looking and cool and I fell for him big time. We started to go out and had such fun around the music scene I thought my life was going to be brilliant. But then we got married. And now it has all turned sad. We have a lovely home, but my husband has stopped playing and started managing other bands instead and he's become just like any other businessman. The excitement's all gone. He wants to be around the house all the time and says he doesn't want to go out because he's with people all the time and wants time at home. But at the end of a hard day (I do flowers for events) I like to relax with friends and a few drinks.

I met the new man when I was out one evening. He's lovely. He's an agent and says he thinks I could be a model. All I can think of is how sexy he is and how exciting my life could be if I was with him. I think I'm in love, but how can I tell? I got it wrong before. Help! My life's in such a mess!

Confused.

Dear Confused

This is normal. I think human beings have a saying, 'to dream the impossible dream'. What they don't add is 'is a recipe for frustration, discontent, unhappiness and letters to problem pages'. You dream a dream, which is something you enjoy doing, and then when someone wakes you up you have the extra thrill of being confused and unhappy. It's a common scenario – if you're human. A sloth would never want that. A sloth prefers not to have problems. So I will hand some of them back to you.

- You say the problem for you is that you don't love your husband any more. Why is this necessarily a problem?
- You say he is kind, thoughtful and lovely, but you don't love him. Why ever not?
- You say he was on TV when you fell in love with him. Is that a good reason to fall in love with someone?
- Was TV an unreal dream and was your parents' life reality?
- You say that your parents were very content together but were boring. Is contentment boring? Sloths think it's bliss.
- Your husband acts like a businessman now because he is a businessman now. It's not a crime. By the way, was your father in business too?
- Modelling? How old are you? Do you seriously believe you could be a model?
- And why would you want to be a model? Do human beings find it attractive to be in the company of etiolated stick insects with knobbly knees and a grumpy look? We eat them.

Poor Confused! That may all seem a bit hard, but sloths are not a sentimental species. And we don't spend our lives beating ourselves up about relationships. We do know how to take it easy, though, and I think you'll find that your life will be much, much more pleasant if you let go of all the expectations of what might be and start to enjoy what's sitting right in front of you a whole lot more. Look around you. Do people really live the way they do on television? Normal people's lives don't have episodes or plot resolution; mostly they just go on, and on a bit more – like sloths. And if they're lucky they enjoy what they get to graze on as they go. But, because you're human you're going to *want some kind of 'solution' to your 'problem', I suppose, so here you are.*

You sell posh flowers. You have a big garden with your lovely house. You and your husband don't do enough together. Grow your own – with your husband. He'll see it as a business opportunity. Believe me. Bedding, dibbling and pricking together will sort you out.

Dear Sloth

I'm not in the habit of writing to papers, or of asking for help with my problems; in fact I don't normally have problems. My life is fine. It's just that something's come up at work. Well, two things actually. A problem with a colleague. And me. I'm perfectly happy at home, and my relationship with my partner's the same as ever, fine. We have two kids at school, she's happy working part-time, and I'm doing well. Very well, in fact, so I don't want to rock any boats. Only this woman started at work recently, and she's been coming on to me ever since. I can't say I'm not flattered; she's very attractive – all the guys say so. She's not at all obvious, though, more Sharon Stone, all tight white shirts and long brown legs. And I just can't help responding. What do I do now? If I give in to temptation (and believe me she is a very tempting prospect) and my partner finds out, I stand to lose the lot. If I hold out, well, all I can say is that doesn't seem like a very tempting prospect at all.

Desperate

Dear Desperate

This is normal. Look around you: all the other guys feel the same way about her; they'd also like to have sex with her. For sloths, sex is natural too. No big deal; it brings babies. But you don't want babies, you just want sex, and to feel that someone finds you attractive, right? Which the other guys don't seem to need. 'Perfectly' happy at home? I don't think so, but people have other things to do than be 'perfectly' happy all the time, so no real problem there – if 'she' weren't around. No problem anyway, in fact. If you have a thick skin and you think it's worth risking everything else, you take the offer of sex and the consequences; if you haven't, you don't. It is that simple.

Oh, and as you know this woman finds you attractive already, and as it's only that and the sex you're after, all that's left to want now is the sex. This is even simpler. Have it with somebody else. Never do it with a work colleague; you might lose access to your leaves. So if you must have sex with someone, try another branch.

Dear Sloth

I'm 14 and very unhappy. I feel a bit like Romeo (I'm studying the play at school). I think I'm in love but my parents don't like the girl I'm going out with. They say I'm too young to go out with anyone but wouldn't mind too much if I joined a youth club with the girl down the road, or something sad like that. Not that Katy's sad. I quite like her really. We used to play together, but that's the problem: she's not grown up. I feel grown up now, and old enough to make my own decisions. And I like Tanya. She's great, really fit and together. She's older than me though (she's 15), and wants me to have sex with her, and I'm not sure about it. Not that I've said so – I don't want her to know because she might think I don't fancy her. I do, but I don't want to have sex, not yet. I think I might be a bit too young. What do you think?

Ryan

Dear Ryan,

You're 14 and very unhappy. This is normal – look around you. You are also rebelling against your parents, which is normal too. As is thinking you are in love with an older woman. When he was a boy, Shakespeare himself thought he was in love with an older woman, and she got him to have sex with her, which meant he had to marry her and leave her his second best bed. I think if he'd written Romeo and Juliet when he was older, he'd have let Romeo marry Katy and live contentedly ever after. You're not going to like this, but sloths learn from their mothers what's going to work best for them. And because they accept what their mothers say, they save themselves a lot of grief (always a good thing for a sloth) and get to live life more as comedy than as tragedy.

Dear Sloth

I've never written to anyone in this way before, so I don't know how to put what I would like to say. I'm not very good at expressing my feelings, as many people tell me. Not unkindly, but they let me know that I'm what they call reserved. I didn't think it was a problem in the past, but now I'm beginning to realise that I've missed out on an awful lot because I haven't stood up for myself. I'm married to a man who also doesn't say very much, but I thought we were happy together. We have two grown-up children who are very good to us and often come to visit, bringing their four children, and we enjoy that very much. We are both 65 by the way. At their last visit one of my grandchildren insisted I tried Friends Reunited for a bit of fun. As a consequence, after 47 years I have met up again with an old schoolfriend, who has made me think much more about my life. I have realised it has amounted to nothing. She has done such exciting things – been married three times and travelled the world. By comparison I have done nothing. I met her for lunch at a rather smart restaurant, the sort I wouldn't usually go to, and we ate such unusual things. When I told my friend I didn't usually experiment because my husband didn't like fancy, spicy food, she became quite cross with me and told me to 'get a life'. She'd had four glasses of wine by that time so I didn't take offence. I think this letter may be starting to ramble, so I'll get to the point. She has suggested that I join her on a cruise and said that we might both 'get lucky'. She also said she didn't imagine my husband would miss me one bit and that I should think of leaving him. Do you think I should?

Reserved

PS We had been thinking of taking a few days in the Lakes (my husband and I).

Dear Reserved

This is normal. It's the zeitgeist (you can Google that if necessary). Brownie points are given for excitement, nul points for taking pleasure in your life. Spice it up as much as you like (or as much as the old lush likes, by the sound of it) but you won't be gaining a life, just a set of casual wear. Up to now you've lived life your way. What's wrong with it? Sounds pretty perfect to me. Of course, if you will compare yourself with a turbo-charged termagant, you lose out a little in the chilli pepper stakes. If not, then look around you. How much luckier do you think you can get?

PS Crawling idly up and down the Lakes, a little local food, just hanging out. Mmmm, that's my kind of cruising.

There are many more problems that our sloth could have considered, but quite frankly they are all much of a muchness:

I have enough to eat and drink, my work's okay, I don't live on the streets, but someone somewhere said that I should define myself by the quality of my relationships, and they are not as perfect as the relationship gods, living on Mount Olympus, say they should be, so I feel a discontented failure. Please tell me how to be a different person, living a different life. And which is the way to Mount Olympus, please?

So our sloth is taking a short zizz.

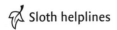

SLOTH HELPLINE NUMBER TWO
– PARENTING

Parenting is nearly as dangerous a territory as relationships. A sloth could get into rather deep water with this one. Heigh-ho.

Children. What are they for?

Does anyone know any more? Once upon a time we had kids because we had sex, and then the kids did a load of work around the place, and then they were our pensions. Or if we were upper class, once upon a time we had kids because we had sex with our cousin, and then the kids didn't do very much, but they did stir themselves to have sex with their cousin, and then we were able to keep everything in the family.

But we all knew what kids were *for*.

Now choice is involved, and keeping the species going is more than just default setting, it's yet another matter of design.

If the world ends it's all Chippendale's fault.

Having a child is now a design statement like any other. It shows we have chosen our own function. By having a child we are no longer simply keeping the species going; now we are keeping 'me' going – me as the agent of a lifestyle, which I have chosen:

> *What is my purpose? Am I to be the facilitator of an enviable international lifestyle and make for myself a fabulous career? In which case having a child wouldn't fit in with the profile I create for myself. Or, on the other hand, am I to style myself on, say, Gwyneth Paltrow and give myself over to earth mother chic with Ecco shoes and an SUV pram? In which case a child will be quite essential.*

It's simply a matter of what we want.

The problem is, though, that half the time we don't know what we want – which lifestyle, which relationship, which persona. Do we choose a boyish man who will himself fulfil all our maternal instincts, or a manly man who wants labradors and kids? Do we choose a girl who wants to party and pursue a career, or one who longs to nest? Or one of the millions of permutations in between? We have so many choices, sometimes it is easiest not to make one at all. In the past, that default would have meant ending up having a baby (how many of us would be here today if our parents or grandparents had enjoyed our degree of choice?), but now, at least for the majority of middle-class women, that default means ending up *not* having a baby.

But then ... the clock ticks on and ... 'Perhaps it would be nice now, after all', and so the next series of choices kicks in. When precisely, what kind of birth, how many babies?

Facts and pre-birth figures

What all this cultural dithering has led to is an extraordinary change in birth habits and birth statistics since choice became the norm. In the early seventies, the average age for giving birth in the UK was 26, and the average for first-time births 23. Just 30 years on, the average ages have risen to 29 and 27, making a drop in birth rate almost inevitable. Indeed, at one point during the 1990s the birth rate fell as low as 1.65 children per woman, not high enough to replace the existing population (and even this level is mostly sustained by younger, poorer, mothers). This trend has recently turned ever so slightly, though, with last year's birth rate rising by 4 per cent, the biggest increase in 25 years. The increase is down to the numbers of women who are having babies considerably later, after the age of 35. The number of mothers over the age of 40 has risen by 10 per cent.

It is often harder for women over 30 to conceive. A proportion of these women will turn to IVF, which brings its own, not entirely desirable consequences, among them the strong possibility of multiple births, which have risen from 12 per thousand births in 1992 to 15 per thousand in 2005, a rise of 25 per cent.

Sadly, it is not a question of the more the merrier, or getting the whole birth thing over and done with in one go once the decision's been made, because the more babies a woman carries, the more risk there is for all of them. For example, when a woman is carrying more than one baby, there is a 50 per cent chance of prematurity, and so a much greater risk of damage and long-term health problems.

Choices like these entail more than simple worry about what to do for the best. Now there's also potentially the subsequent guilt of having made a choice that has led to harm. At least in the past you could always blame fate. Now we have to bear the burden of being the authors of our own destiny.

Delivering the goods

However much guilt we might feel at certain times and over certain things, we can also be quite unscrupulous where our kids are concerned. In earlier times a baby was born and *then* its potential as a psychological and emotional tool (in social one-up-manship or the manipulation of a relationship for example) might have been spotted by the diligent parent. Today it may well be created especially to fit such a purpose – to be a companion, a prize exhibit, a generator of social security benefits, or perhaps simply to fulfil 'my right to a child'.

There's a sense in which, rather than children being dependent on their parents, modern parents have become dependent on their children. They can provide status, a lifestyle and vicarious fulfilment. Most of all, though they offer us one of the greatest spending and decorating opportunities in the world.

According to popular journalistic reports, these days it costs £300,000 to raise a child in London, and it's easy to see why if you take a look at the glossy magazines. From SUV pushchairs, to off-road mini quad bikes, from fairy castle fourposters to freaky forest dens, from baby bear all-in-ones to the latest football strip, there aren't any childhood 'needs' that can't be – expensively – met via website, catalogue or shopping mall. We can spend thousands of pounds, if we are so inclined, recreating full-on infant fantasies in the privacy of our own homes. But, sadly, these will last only until our little moppet turns into a monster itself and makes the decision that purply-black grunge is now the way to go, and, no, you are not allowed in there to do it yourself, because it's private. Go away.

And we let them, don't we? We let them speak to us like that because we've lost the confidence to deny them anything, especially the right to free speech (theirs, but most definitely not ours).

The modern 'business' of childcare has become less and less to do with taking care of children and more and more to do with taking care of what other people think. And why? It's the same story as with relationships:

- We have lost touch with the ways our families did things (which, by and large, worked well enough).
- We have become overly reliant on 'expert' advice – which has chopped and changed between breast and bottle, terry and disposable, freedom and boundaries. So what do they know?

- We believe more in the media versions of parenting and family life than we do in what we can actually see happening around us.
- We expect nothing less than perfectibility.
- Our lives – and our children's lives – are full of speed and over-stimulation.
- We have become extremely competitive, especially where our children's achievements are concerned.

Perfect pa(re)nts

In middle-class child-rearing, perfection comes as standard, of course, but then we have to endeavour to be more perfect than the other full-time working parents we are in competition with – who are also working hard to outperform everyone else.

I don't Know How She Does It isn't just the title of a novel; the phrase is also the secret psychological 'upper' of thousands of high-flying professional women who probably spent serious time writing perfect university theses on the domestic slavery of the Victorian wife. Over-achieving makes us feel good; it makes us feel smug – especially in comparison with those unambitious, unfulfilled stay-at-home women. They are the ones who have so much time on their hands but so much to live up to that, according to *Perfect Madness*, Judith Warner's book on motherhood in America, they've turned into 'helicopter mothers', always hovering 'caringly' over their children. The situation is not obviously different for some stay-at-home mothers in Britain either.

Not to obsess on perfect parenting would mean to be without a role, to be, in effect, nobody. I mean what's the point of us if we 'have nothing to do'? (Can you hear a sloth chortle?) So, if we are at home with the kids, there must be some pretty conspicuous, child-centred, frenzied activity going on to prove we are fulfilling our function and doing okay, mustn't there? Like making sure the baby gets stimulated to the point of multi-colour, multi-sensory spontaneously combusting friction. And making sure we get to the double yellow lines on the bend outside the school on time so that some other mother won't get there before us and risk running our kid down. Then we must get the brood home in time to practice the violin and do their homework before we pop them in the car and take them off for their keep-fit class. But what we must never, ever do under any circumstances is leave them to their own devices. There are three reasons for this:

1. They might get hurt if they: risk riding their bikes on their own; experiment with weapons ingeniously made from things found in the neighbour's garden shed; experiment with the neighbour (who is bound to be a pervert, take pictures of the kids in the nude and then leave their bodies in the bushes, even though, according to the British National Society for the Protection of Children, while 63 per cent of people believe most murdered children are killed outside the home, in truth 80 per cent of them are killed by their own parents).

2. They might develop survival skills of their own and make us feel redundant. (But then Newton's interest in physics developed out of boredom and childhood parental neglect, and he turned into a massive, world-class over-achiever – though a little mad – so it's a close call).

3. They might lie about in the grass, chewing the cud (metaphorically), and playing at whatever they feel like, leading to indolence, lack of direction, sunburn and Isaac Newton (see point 2 above).

Perfectionism is a tyranny necessitating unbelievably, unslothfully, unnecessarily hard work.

Rude kids rule KO?

But, of course, the tyranny described above is a particular species, one that exercises control over a particular section of the middle classes. Because we are in such a perfectly confused state over what children are for, there's also another kind of tyranny at work, which is more than a little at odds with the previous one. This is the one that says the kids rule okay! And that, as parents who are paying for their upkeep (and usually letting them keep most of their earnings on the side, instead of giving them a very valuable lesson in economics and saving them from a lifetime in debt), we have no right WHATSOEVER to control what they do, when they do it, where they do it and in whose company. Furthermore, and notwithstanding any personal interest, emotional or financial, we also have no right whatsoever to control what any young person does in public or private, however grievously their doings may infringe our or our neighbours' right to any substantial enjoyment of our only foreseeable time on this earth (the sloth has a little something to say on that later).

We have become a little too detached from an inheritance that declared, 'Children should be seen and not heard' and rather too dependent on the theories of child 'experts' who tell us that children's voices *must* be heard.

The consequences of the tolerant approach many of us have felt compelled to take – not necessarily because it always seemed instinctively right but often because it seemed like the easier or more socially approved option – have, ironically, not always been great for the kids concerned, especially when they have meant that kids have ended up with even more of what they've 'wanted'. Because this kind of indulgence hasn't resulted in time spent lying in the grass or up a tree, but in lots of television, lots of sweets, lots of internet and computer games, lots of magazines, lots of time when 'It's none of your business what I do, get out of my face', and lots and lots of time when they're out and about like lonely little Lords of Misrule, all topsy-turvy and giddy with limitlessness.

It's very tricky getting the right balance between over- and under-involvement with children, just as it is between over- and under-expectation. It's something that lucky people learn from growing up properly in the first place, and that most often comes free inside with good (enough) parenting.

For the rest of us there's neglect (not even a slothful first resource) or taking on advice from all comers, with the consequent happy outcome of yet more *choice* – hooray!

More happily still, there is another way!

Dear Sloth

Yes, it's that helpline again.

Dear Sloth

I'm in despair. My little boy, who is just over two, is becoming so difficult. I know people talk about the terrible twos, but I wasn't expecting it to be quite like this, especially as he's always seemed rather delicate. He was a nervy baby, colicky and very bad at sleeping, and we still seem to have him in bed with us more often than not. I suppose I have spoilt him a little as, so far, he is our only child and we waited a long time for him. He's always caused us a bit of a worry over feeding – he's slow and fussy – but I've been very careful to make sure he's had plenty of vitamins, and since he's been on solids he's always had organic baby food. But I'm really concerned that he's not growing properly because he just doesn't seem to want to eat. I've tried everything the health visitor has recommended and the books say, but he still just throws his food around. I don't know what more I can do to encourage him.

And nearly as bad as the trouble over his eating is the trouble I'm having with him over his nappies. I've been very careful over his potty training, as I didn't want him to have phobias and become retentive, so I've tried to encourage him by making potty time play time, but he's just not being co-operative. In fact it's worse than that; he's getting so naughty he won't go on the pot at all, and he's started to play with the poo in his nappies (once he even tried to eat it – I was so worried it would be toxic). What can I do? My husband, who has been brilliant up to now, is beginning to lose patience with the situation and says he's just being naughty and I should get things into perspective. But I'm not sure how to, and anyway I still think we should be careful in case there's something wrong. Please can you help me?

Despairing

Dear Despairing

This is normal. It's what happens when you spend more time worrying than sleeping. You have everything back to front. You say he was a nervy colicky baby, but where did he learn this from? You. What would happen if you stopped worrying? Would your baby eat less? No. Would he not sleep as well? No. Would he do more than go through the motions when potty training? No. So, although I don't normally like to give advice because that generally means giving people more things to do, this one is easy because it means giving you less things to do. Drop the worry; it just takes too much out of you. Anyway, your kid is normal. How do I know? The health visitor would have told you if he weren't. Look around you. Is he like other two-year-olds? Yes. And a tough little nut by the sound of it. You should be pleased. (Question: if not, why not?) Read less, sleep more (but leave the kid in his own bed) and be thankful you've got such a committed little green recycler.

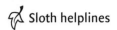

Dear Sloth

I really don't know what to do about my daughter. She was such a lovely, happy, friendly little girl until she went to secondary school two years ago, and then she seemed to change. It happened when she got in with a group of girls who would probably have been called 'the wrong crowd' in the past. As it was about the same time that her father and I were splitting up, I didn't notice what was going on in quite the usual way. The other girls are all fixated on boys, couldn't care less about school work and seem free from any parental control. And now my daughter's getting like them – bad-tempered, rude (especially to me), aggressive – and she dresses in a way that (and again this sounds so old-fashioned) quite frankly is provocative. It's not overt, like boob tubes and heels, but she's taken to wearing grunge torn in inappropriate places and half-transparent where it isn't torn. The other thing is she never washes, just sprays herself with something strong and cheap-smelling and then plasters on more make-up before going out. I can't talk to her father about it (he'll say it's all my fault), my mother's away in Australia, and I know the school won't take any responsibility for what the girls get up to out of hours. How can I get my lovely daughter back?

Concerned

Dear Concerned

You depend on your daughter more than she depends on you. Look around you; her behaviour is normal. For sloths it's different, our young depend on us, we don't depend on them (anyway there's always another in the pipeline). They are cute, though, a bit like your daughter, and so we take care of them. Your daughter has stopped being cute and started to move away. She's put a foot out onto the branch, and at that point a sloth would think to itself, 'I like you, but you fall, you fall'. Tear a few tough leaves out of the sloth's book of childcare:

- Parents know the best sources of lifetime nourishment – make sure she does her schoolwork.

- Who wants to be cute at fourteen?

- Looking a little unkempt is fine; at times, dare I say it, even rather appealing (that'll stop her), but never neglect personal hygiene – it's a shower or else.

- Sticks and stones ... (when and why did that saying go out of circulation?) Ignore your daughter's rudeness when it's only directed at you; she's cross with you and you can take it. When she's rude to someone else, push her off the branch.

- When there's nothing more you can do, tuck your head under, grab a branch, and let her go. If you got it right in the early stages, she won't go far.

Dear Sloth

I think I know the answer you're going to give me, but I'll ask you all the same. Should I go back to work after having my baby? I'm sure you'll say that it'll be much easier not to and that no one should work harder than they have to in life, but I thought I'd ask you anyway. I'm stuck somewhere between what my boyfriend thinks and what my mother thinks at the moment, and don't really know what I think myself. You seem the perfect person (is that right? – 'animal' seems so, oh I don't know ... offensive, somehow) to ask. I'm 26 and really quite keen on developing my career as far as I can. I work in HR and would like to take all the exams I can and one day have my own business. I also like to have financial independence. But, and it's a big one, I'd also like to be a good mother and be there for my kids when they have sports days and perhaps even sometimes when they get home from school. How can I do both? My mother says she never had any qualms about giving her job up for us, and look how we turned out (not much I can say to that, is there?). My boyfriend says it's all right for her; my father had a well paid job and houses cost less than an egg and bacon sandwich then. I know they're both right in their way, and I also know I would go mad stuck at home if I had no stimulation, but why should I let other people see my kids' first steps? How can I get it right?

Vacillating

PS My boyfriend really has quite a good job, but we have a mortgage the size of the moon and I would still like to see a bit more of the world.

Dear Vacillating

Oh dear, all this agonising is so terribly, terribly normal. And it's so very now. How many people are you? How many lives do you have? How many questions can you think of? Still, at least you've taken the plunge and aren't asking whether you should have kids at all (far too exhausting to go into). I suppose we sloths are fortunate because our homes cost even less than a bacon and egg sandwich, but that's down to us not feeling a primordial need to do DIY, as we have better ways of spending our time. All the same, there are ways of getting around this situation. Notice, I do not say 'solve this problem'; this is not a problem, it is NFYP: Normal For Young Professionals. (Young amateurs seem not to find themselves in a similar situation.) For we sloths, flexibility is the key to getting what we want, so:

Way 1: the way to keep your boyfriend happy. Go back to work and earn shedloads of money. Employ a terrifically pretty Croatian au pair and then you can either a) sulk all you like all day for missing out on the kids, because he'll never notice, or b) go off to Peru while he bravely 'holds the fort' (and probably the au pair).

Way 2: the way to keep your mother happy. She's right, of course: there's no substitute for either good maternal care or the easy option. So once you've given up work and been evicted, the obvious way around your housing difficulty is for all three of you to move in with mother. Voila!

Way 3: the way to be happy yourself. You would like to be around in the day to watch your child's precious developmental milestones and yet still have financial independence, chic clothes and a little stimulation. The clear choice is to work from home. Your boyfriend can't afford to be fussy about what you do, can he?

If that isn't very helpful, perhaps it's because there isn't any help to be had. Sloths don't have a problem because sloths don't want to have it all. What monkey thought that excessively busy idea up? Look around you: do you really see lots and lots of perfect people keeping all of it together all of the time? Or just a lot of people muddling through, getting some bits right and most bits so, so? You have to make choices – no-one has it all. Where did you learn to think they do? From the television?

PS Good luck when the baby comes, and remember, when sloths need to boost their energy reserves they have a little bask in the sun.

Dear Sloth

I've had just about enough and am thinking of leaving my wife. She was a perfectly normal woman, with a job and a life, until she had our son, now aged two. We had a perfectly normal relationship, too, with sex from time to time. Now, because of the baby – no, he's no longer a baby, he's a boy – because the boy's in our bed every night, there's no chance at all, and she doesn't seem to realise what that means for a man. I've tried my best to be supportive, but there's no end to her worries. As soon as one problem looks as though it's getting sorted out, another one pops up out of the woodwork. It's potty training now, but what next? I can see no end to it. Is there any way to let her know how this is affecting me without seeming selfish and uncaring?

Fed Up

Dear Fed Up

You could let her know that if this goes on, eventually your son will be forced to kill you and marry her, and see what she chooses. Or you could just take him back to his own bed yourself – and then tell her that what you are going to do next will help her sleep.

Have you noticed that the majority of those letters came from women? No fiction, no biased selection, that was proportional representation. It seems that women still have to do the majority of worrying about kids, even if(!) everything else is shared. Which the sloth says is just about normal, and adds, 'Just look around you.'

SLOTH HELPLINE NUMBER THREE
– HOMES AND GARDENS

'Have nothing in your home that you do not know to be useful, or believe to be beautiful,' said William Morris, but, sadly, not to the manufacturers of fondue sets, windchimes and chimeneas.

Ever since the beginnings of design (see page 26) we've been at the mercy of other people's ideas of good taste. It's bad enough when it's just our neighbours' tastes that we have to respond to ('Oh, yes, of course I do. It's er ... really very striking, isn't it?'), but it's much more difficult when it comes to professional taste, especially when it's fed to us via the media. Then it's the same old story. What we come across on TV or in a book or magazine we take much more seriously than what comes from our nearest and dearest, whose sanity we'd be more than happy to dispute. I mean, whatever my immediate (and obviously untutored) impressions, perhaps that corrugated iron, breezeblock and black glass replacement for the derelict Georgian terrace that I saw on the latest TV design programme really is cutting-edge. And, yeah, I think blue glass balls and shingle are like totally now and will be really low-maintenance after the lawn, but largely because some designer on the TV says so.

If we hadn't learnt to doubt the evidence of just about everything we've ever personally known and understood – about ourselves, our taste, our preferred habits and, well, just about everything – how would we ever have allowed the 1960s? I blame Thomas Chippendale. If he hadn't invented design, we would never have put ourselves in the hands of people who had no more sense than a newt but did have access to passports. They were the ones who, having seen somewhere like Cordoba, briefly, came away from it convinced that Britain was just gagging for a similar plaza lifestyle. And so they popped a few expansive pencil sketches, decorated with merely a soupçon of shrubbery and human life, in to the planners' office, and lo and behold, out popped Crawley, Basingstoke and Milton Keynes, England's most up-to-date (and ugly) towns.

Such towns may owe a little bit to planning radicals who felt we should be able to plan our way out of the dirty, crowded Victorian slums, such as the modernist Le Corbusier (though what he personally wanted us to live in was a giant machine in the sky), but they owe far more to the eternal belief that 'experts' somehow know more about the conditions of our lives than we do. So architects and town planners feel free to play about with the way we should live (and live out their dreams and fantasies). They plonk us down wherever it suits their latest ideology, in whatever is the latest wonder material, which could be anything from asbestos to reinforced concrete. But how come they themselves always seem to end up living in surprisingly beautiful, traditional, stone-built homes?

Stage-set living

Is there anything to choose between an architect's drawing and a stage design? Neither has the remotest sense of context, human or otherwise. And they both transport us just as readily to India as to Idaho, to Gothic horror as to classical unity. And in both cases we are daft enough to agree, very, very willingly, to suspend our disbelief, which is why wibbly-wobbly, weather-conscious English towns like Croydon have over time uncomplainingly allowed themselves to be redesigned as wind tunnels, and why someone, somewhere, once went along with the idea of tower blocks. But architect's drawings and stage designs are so addictively fulfilling, the hit is instant, and that's so very modern. Not for them the slow organic evolution of what came about through people's way of living.

It's not fair to blame architects entirely, though. We have all fallen for the magic idea that we can easily be something different from what we've ever been. We nearly all believe in the possibility of the instantaneous reconfiguration of all that has been into all that might be. All that's needed to turn our lives around into a dramatic new reality is a dramatic new stage set.

We can all do the exotic re-invention, too, as long as we have access to a TV set or a magazine rack. A few quick flicks of the remote control or the magazine's pages and, lo and behold, a new backdrop, a new style, a new life, a new me.

So what shall I be today?

I think I fancy being a rustic Provençal. I can be free, I can have the load of my everyday English life lifted and I can become all exotic and foreign, bronzed, authentic, organic. All it will take is a few deft decorating touches and a shopping trip to Fired Earth, Faience and Kitchens, and my home will soon be lazing in the heat of the sunlight, midst shade-dappled, vine-strewn terraces. I just need to buy:

- One sun-bleached, rough-hewn table.

- Some rich red terracotta tiles, on which the aforementioned table will stand four-square.
- Some thick, naive, pottery that can be filled with husky wine and glistening oil-steeped olives.
- One eccentric straw basket, from which crusty bread that begs to be broken can spill.
- One rustic fruit bowl.
- One thick stook of lavender stalks, charmingly tied with raffia.

And away I go, tripping laughingly through the olive groves.

We can buy into a prefabricated fantasy carefully prepared for us by a style guru or we can re-invent ourselves according to our own internally generated fantasies, borrowing bits from this film and that advert. After all, perhaps it's best not to limit the scope of what we might become by committing too firmly to only one stylistic statement. So we can bring a little cosmopolitan style into the Tuscan countryside, or space-age technology into the refurbishment of a wharfside tobacco warehouse, or a sophisticated touch to the re-interpretation of the rural Dorset idyll. It's all so easy. It just requires the little light trick of a Warhol Monroe print on the rustic walls here, a Venetian chandelier over the ball-and-claw bath there, a sheet of zinc just about anywhere. And don't forget the suggestive possibilities of an artful pile of early Penguin paperbacks; a row of pastel, graduated files or a dinky set of handcuffs. There's a perfect little detail that will echo everything we want our interiors to say about us just waiting in some perfect little boutique down a perfect little side road in some perfect little town.

Banishing the past

Whether it's that earthy peasant chic or laid-back urban cool, once we have the perfect backdrop, surely the perfect life will follow too. But only if we never renege on the fittings, banishing mahogany from our Clerkenwell space, never allowing chintz to darken the door of our loft apartment and erasing every shred of Formica from our cottage. From now on let there only be co-ordinates – unless, of course, we're after the wonderful wittiness of the eclectic mix, the humour of a designer gnome stool twinned with Victorian whatnots and flying ducks on the wall. Even then, perish the thought that we might find a home for anything that has actually been passed down to us. It's so much more *now* to pick it up in that little shop where they sell all kinds of wonderful things.

It's all most unsloth-like. Not only is there all that Herculean mental, physical and psychological effort involved in the repeated restyling (no-o-o-o-o-o, not again), which is so foreign to a creature that lives and breathes relaxation, but there's also the loss of a sloth-like enjoyment in picking up learning from what we've inherited, which is weird because we all love to go to heritage museums (well, perhaps our children have to be dragged there) and repeat the mantras of, 'However did they manage?' and 'I bet that's worth a fortune now'. But that doesn't always seem to translate into wanting to gain knowledge and experience from the things we had the chance to hang on to ourselves.

Rarely nowadays do we hear sentences such as, 'Granny used to bake her famous rhubarb and apple pie in this', as a battered enamel pie dish is pulled out from the back of a cupboard before being used to keep the tradition going on into the next generation; and, 'I know it's a bit of a mess, but it is family and it's absolutely the best chair I've found to feed the baby in', as a new family heirloom gets broken in one more time. And what about the old tools that have already stood the test of time with Dad – the ones that genuinely won't shatter when they hit the wall rather than the nail, that can actually be sharpened rather than having to be replaced at financial and environmental expense? Should anyone feel free to call themselves a recycling devotee if they throw a workable thing away simply because it doesn't look right? Just ask your nearest sloth.

A house is for living

Can a house be called a home if nobody can really use it? Once upon a time, a house was primarily for living in, not for looking at, and what it ended up looking like was an echo of what it did. Examples are some of the wonderful artists' studios on the A4 highway into London or the weavers' cottages in Bradford on Avon, in the south-west of England. Can we really say that modern houses are there for us and for what we need to do in them, or are we now at the beck and call of what our houses (and the people who planned them) will allow us to do in them? Take the woman who commissioned, at huge expense, a Modernist glass house and found it dictated every detail of how she lived. She said the house was so perfect, and so perfectly exposed, that even a coat hanger looked like an alien object hell bent on messing it up. No sooner had she moved in than she moved right out again.

That may be an extreme example, but these days there are many less ambitious houses around, belonging to apparently sane and social human beings, in which there is no longer any prospect of sitting in guilt-free comfort on the carefully plumped up sofa cushions, or of disturbing a precisely arranged Starck implement in order actually to cook, or (and this one *really* gets beyond the pain barrier of the sloth) of being able to excavate down as far as the business part of a bed, beneath the overwhelming avalanche of bolsters, teddy bears and throws. And then whatever happened to our love affair with animals? A cat or dog has to take its dignity in its paws in today's house before it attempts the perilous crossing of a wood-effect floor.

We seem to have forgotten that houses are for living in and not just for the Christmas issue.

No escape

It's not over when we get to the back door either, because then there's the little matter of the rash of TV garden makeovers to contend with. These persuasive programmes have left a generation of TV addicts believing that not only is garden re-design an essential fact of life, but that it should take place every bit as instantly as interior re-design, if not, in fact, a little faster. Which is hardly surprising considering that it involves pretty much the same elements of 'rooms', wiring, water, timber, carpentry, cement, heating, and the ever-present, all-embracing imported plants in pots. The house has moved outdoors; it's just a pity that no-one told the weather. But why should anyone concern themselves with the damp and cold reality when instant gardening can be the same kind of triumph of fantasy over function as instant homemaking, with the addition of space heaters.

Little evidence remains that gardens are anything more than a stage set. Where are the once common food sources? The apple trees, the raspberries, the tomatoes and rows of beans – the greenhouses even? Gardens always used to be at least a little bit about food. Now all we seem to want them to feed is the eye. We don't want to have to spend time working in the garden (bear with this one, says the sloth), we want to be able to fantasise ourselves sitting in it with a glass of something in our hand (no problem so far) just like we do abroad ... so we want it to look like a Mediterranean room, with timber floors, large terracotta pots, pretty glass and metal furniture (with cushions) and gravel everywhere. And we want to be able to sit there quickly too.

Well, forgive a stupid sloth, but where's the long-term ease in that? It's just like indoors: hard work to keep the stage set up to scratch, and if we let any of it get used at all, or even just leave it to nature's tender mercy, the whole contrived thing starts to look a mess. The timber decking, the pergolas and the trellis start to rot; the plants in their clay prisons shrivel and wither; the furniture stains and rusts; the cushions (always forgotten) go damp and musty; and the gravel collects leaves and mush. Five years down the line (and how many of these 'effort-free' efforts won't need re-inventing before that time), the lovely Mediterranean room ends up looking, well, rather sorry for itself. If we want to keep it up we have to work, work, work.

The really lazy garden

When we do go on holiday to the genuine Mediterranean, do we really choose to spend our time in outdoor rooms, or do we actually find it much more delightful to laze around out of the heat of the midday sun under some ancient untidy tree in an unkempt, dusty olive grove? An equal, now almost forgotten, charm could once be found in a half-neglected, home-grown English garden. Long grass and all, these gardens looked like nature's teatime treat, full of rambling flowers, pretty weeds, insects, butterflies and hidey holes that children turned into whatever fantasy world they chose. Where do children play untidily in made-over outdoor rooms, in which grass has been tidied away and exchanged for gravel? Where can they build their dens, dream and hide out from Mum and Dad? Especially if Mum and Dad have already organised their play spaces for them, buying in the equipment from the garden centre or over the internet, in bright primary colours or solid green oak?

The really lazy way of life

Strange though it may seem, having a garden rather than a 'space' can save us an awful lot of effort in the most unexpected ways.

- Those of us who actually enjoy the business side of gardening can save ourselves the trouble, time and expense of going to the gym by working out with a spade and a fork, and we can be pretty sure that nobody's going to get us all steamed up by hogging the best equipment.

- Those of us who'd rather die than swing a strimmer can spend our time swinging from a hammock in our own little wildlife haven, peacefully smug that we are doing something to save the planet.

- Those of us who are concerned about the environment can grow indigenous plants and vegetables, and so decrease our carbon footprint without too much effort.
- Those of us who need therapy will find it freely available in a weeding session – no cost, no need to learn a foreign language.
- And those of us who just love life can find it all in our own back garden.

Sloths were possibly in William Morris's mind when he said his bit about having nothing around us that we do not know to be useful or believe to be beautiful. They worked this out – or something similar – thousands of years before him. Of course, beauty is always in the eye of the beholder, but sloths find green things beautiful, and a lot of people are beginning to think along the same lines. If you aren't among them, then this particular Sloth helpline may not be for you, but if you are, then you may find it covers something rather more than you expected.

Dear Sloth

So let's see what the sloth has to say about all of this.

Dear Sloth

I have a dream. I want to build a house for our future. I've been watching a number of programmes about property buying and building and I'm sure it's the only way forward for me and my family. Old houses never seem to update well, most modern estate houses are too small in the first place, and what I really want is for my family to grow up in something a bit memorable and special. I have many DIY skills and know that there's a lot of work I could do myself in the evening and at weekends without having to pay over the odds for it. Other work I could pay for out of salary and the sale of our flat – I'm certain of that. All that is needed is a decent plot of land, which we could fund by the sale of my recently deceased parents' house, so money shouldn't be a problem.

My wife and I have discussed this, and she agrees that we could survive in a caravan while the build went on. The children are quite small, three and six, so they will probably look on it all as a bit of an adventure. The house I want to build would make any short-term inconvenience worthwhile, because it would, in fact, be more than just a bit special. It's essentially a series of steel and glass cubes linked by glazed walkways at first floor level – a piece of modern sculpture. I'd like to think I would be creating a statement for the future, one that could become my children's inheritance.

Do you think this is a wise move?

Dreamer

Dear Dreamer

This ambition is normal for someone who has watched too much TV. The first questions that spring to mind are: 'Have you ever worked in a canning factory?' and 'Are your children pilchards?' The next is: 'What was your father's dream?' Perhaps he wanted to bring up his family in a home, not a dream.

These are not very kind questions, but sloths aren't dreamers and don't do sentiment. And perhaps your wife won't when she has to struggle over the winter months to look after small children in a caravan. And, yes, it will run over the winter months and, no, your children will not think it's an adventure much beyond the first few weeks. Children have a very short attention span; look around you if you haven't already noticed. In fact, they may soon forget they have a father, as they will hardly see you, lost in your own dreams. I think, by and large, they would prefer the more ordinary inheritance of a bit of ordinary time spent with an ordinary daddy and with an unstressed mummy. Question answered?

Dear Sloth

I'm worried about my little boy. He won't eat anything but burgers and chips. I can't get him to touch vegetables at all – he says they taste yuck. He's also unhappy at school and says it's all boring. I think he's too young at eight to be so fed up with everything and, having watched Jamie Oliver, I think there might be a connection with his diet. I want to try him on different foods, but how can I make him eat better things? He just says no.

Trying Hard

Dear Trying Hard

This is normal for a modern parent – and orginally your letter was sent to the parenting section, but it fits nicely here and kills two birds with one stone (hopefully both harpy eagles). The answer lies in your garden. Look around you: how many miserable gardeners do you see? Give your little boy a patch to grow vegetables in all by himself and see if he doesn't come over all jolly green giant. He'll want to eat what he's grown, he'll get fit and healthy, and he'll develop an interest in science, all at the same time. No sweat.

Dear Sloth

We thought we'd write to you together, as ours is a bit of a joint problem.

We both love luxury and comfort, and have been having fun decorating our Victorian garden flat together. We really wanted to turn it into a bit of an exotic fantasy, all wall hangings and rugs, with the souvenirs we've picked up on our travels around North Africa and Turkey providing the theme. We've bought fat sofas and cushions and thought it would all be decadent and sensual and we'd throw great parties, but – and it's a big but ... in fact a great big pain in the butt – we've started sneezing and wheezing, and the doctor says it must be down to mould spores. We've looked behind the hangings and under a rug, and found it – mould. Now it seems we're allergic to our home. What can we do?

Two Snufflers

Dear Snufflers

This is normal. Victorian houses are damp. Now, in general, I'm not averse to some healthy algae – I find it helps to have a few different life forms in the system – but in your case it doesn't suit. So? It seems you will have to do one of two things:

Accept defeat. Look around you – this house is in control. Do what it insists: put trainers on the cat and wood-effect on the floor. Buy buckets of bleach and clean up the rest of your act.

Sell up and have your fantasy in a bright modern flat instead – or in exotic Africa.

Dear Sloth

I have built my wife a beautiful new kitchen but she insists on cluttering it up with recycling boxes. It's meant to be a streamlined and efficient galley but half the time you can't walk down the central passage without bashing your shins to pieces. I say just chuck the lot into the normal bin. She says we must consider the environment, so the room gets filled up with smelly milk cartons and empty vegetable tins. It's playing havoc with my environment. How environmentally conscious do you think she is really being leaving all this junk about?

Eco Terrorist

Dear Eco Terrorist

How refreshing to get your letter, but sadly this is normal. People like to feel they are doing what they call 'their bit' for the environment. Even though:

- Recycling vans go improbable distances (using fuel) to collect tiny amounts of materials.
- Most of the glass is recycled into tarmac.
- Carbon emissions from stationary vehicles waiting to get past the vans rise as sky-high as the drivers' tempers.

Look around you – you'll find it's not just your wife. But don't run away with the idea that sloths are anti-recycling; we've been doing it for thousands of years – in fact, we probably invented the word. I won't go into sordid details, but the trick to getting it right is, first, to limit your by-products, and second, to bury them. That way you get the most wonderful outcome in the world: compost. (Sloths have a thing about compost.)

Let your wife know you have been taking advice from a hoary old environmentalist (naming no names) and that you have found a cleaner way forward, which will suit your tidy nature very nicely, too. Buy your milk in bottles, and everything else in as little packaging as possible. Bury everything leftover in a lovely tidy compost box and then use it to grow your own vegetables. Blissfully easy.

Which all rather economically leads us into the next Sloth helpline.

SLOTH HELPLINE NUMBER FOUR
– CONSUMERISM

According to a recent American study, compulsive shoppers may have a dysfunction of the orbito-frontal cortex, a part of the brain just behind the eyes that is involved in decision-making. The research was done using monkeys but most probably applies to people too(!), and shows that choice, which involves a change of natural preference, may well be influenced in strange ways by any damage, even slight, to neurons in that part of the brain. Basically, the orbito-frontal cortex fails to balance competing demands from other parts of the brain and goes into overdrive. The researchers say there may well be a number of outcomes, one of the main ones being that people can no longer reject unnecessary products.

At the same time, we hear that 9.2 billion plastic bottles have to be disposed of every year in the UK, and that the British drink 1,490 million litres of water out of such bottles, the manufacture of which requires 220,000 barrels of oil. (Mmmm, tasty, no wonder sloths gave water up.) Much of this water will travel 600 miles to arrive on the shop shelf.

We have taps.

Do these facts alone mean that the entire British population is disturbed in the orbito-frontal regions?

Here's another interesting little fact. By Easter Sunday of this year, the United Kingdom had used up all its annual national productivity, meaning that from then on all its goods would have to be imported. If every country behaved like this, we would need three whole planets to keep us all going in the style to which those of us in the Western world have become accustomed.

How is it that these days we see nothing remotely daft in first driving to the gym to get fit (for what?), then driving to the healthfood store to buy the vitamin C (in the tube which we will then recycle) that we could have ingested from grazing off the hedgerows we passed while out on our health-giving, environmentally friendly walk. Then we vote Green.

Race to the till

Feeling unwell, unhappy, unloved? Try a little retail therapy. It's bound to do you good – all the good in the world. It's just another sign of our schizo society. We all want to save the planet – doesn't everyone? – but at the same time we also want to have a perfect home, a perfect sound system and a perfect wardrobe. It has been estimated that the average woman spends £80,000 on shoes in her lifetime – and how many of us think that one coat will do, or one TV, or one car even? We throw sofas out when we change our colour scheme, and we update technology whenever something new is advertised.

This isn't a rant in favour of stopping spending and turning hippy – apart from anything else, the world would come to a grinding halt, and even a sloth goes faster than that; it's a long hard look at the absurdities of our current purchasing compulsion. I mean, when all's said and done, does it actually make us feel all that good? Isn't it, rather, just another way in which we make ourselves feel inadequate? How can any of us keep up in the race for bargains, bargains, bargains – clip out coupons, save a fortune; 'Have you got your saver card?'; 'Don't miss the sale of a lifetime'; double blue stars, but only if you come on Sunday; air miles with this, bonus points with that ... and perhaps the scariest of all, 'Don't worry, you needn't miss out, take away £2,000 of credit with our card TODAY!' At the time of writing, the British population owes £56.35 billion pounds on credit cards – and this amount is increasing by £1,000,000 every four minutes. If that isn't a cause for anxiety, we must be in denial.

As with any addiction, we're so busy chasing the future hit that we've given up asking ourselves whether we're enjoying where we're at now. There's the constant sense that we're missing out on something better, that we haven't made the most of some fantastic opportunity and that we should be doing (and spending) more, more, more to keep ourselves up to speed. Consumerism is really yet another way of telling ourselves that we are currently in the failure camp.

Bargain travel

We are also, currently, never, ever, where we want to be. Consumerism has hit travel, too. We can have another kind of perfect life if only we can go to the perfect places we can see in the brochures and on TV. In the UK, approximately 43,000,000 trips are made abroad each year. People from Oxford think that Heidelburg is the perfect place to be, and people from Heidelburg think Oxford is the absolute best ... And once we get there, what do we do? We watch one another being tourists. We go to Spain for the Spanish way of life, Giverny for the inspiration of the garden, Greece for the wonders of the ancient world, and what we get is, mainly, more of us. Which rather tends to lessen the effect of 'foreign'.

It all comes down, once again, to our worshipping at the shrine of instant. Rather than taking time over travel, and getting to know the places on the way, we want to be there, do it, and get back home again, often several times a year. Holidays are now just another form of mass production – throw this one away and buy another one. By the time we've driven to the airport carpark, taken the bus to the terminal, lined up at the check-in desk, walked through the scanners, waited in loading, strapped ourselves in on the plane and drunk ourselves calmer, it's a wonder we realise we've been anywhere foreign at all. The whole process is so exhausting that by the time it's over we need another break to get over it.

The other man's grass (and bread and cheese)

Perhaps if we could slow down just a bit and ask ourselves what it is we are really looking for, we might find greater profit in the luxury of time. As it is, we end up on the treadmill of more, quicker, cheaper that leads to the loss of anything that can't compete, which inevitably means small, local, personal. In one village in Somerset, England, seven good local shops have closed in ten years: a butcher's, a baker's, a grocery, a greengrocery, a hardware store, a wool and craft shop and a post office. The bank and the petrol station went too. If there's no time to stop as we shop, perhaps it's germane to wonder what we're going to do with the time we've saved – drive home along the busy roads to spend essential time watching TV ads that will tell us how friendly and cheap the 'local' superstore is, perhaps? Or plan our next holiday in that more relaxed foreign country where they know how to live properly – real shops, fresh food and all that?

If our orbito-frontal cortexes are getting confused, it's no wonder. We're all trying to do much too much. Our poor little brains have forgotten what it feels like to stop at one choice and enjoy the pleasure that might be got out of that one thing we've chosen. Perhaps we should bear in mind the village in Africa visited by some Western bigwigs recently. When asked what the children would like to be given as souvenirs of the VIPs' visit, the village elders replied, 'Pencils, rubbers and rulers', not only because these things were needed, but also because there was nothing the children liked more than to be able to draw. They could have chosen anything and it would have been made available, but these simple things were what they wanted.

If we must be consumers, and it looks as if we must, at least let us enjoy what we are consuming with a bit more relish. At the moment it seems that we are throwing most of it away. In Britain alone, 28.2 million tonnes of rubbish are chucked out every year. That's seven times the body weight of the British population, at a rate that would fill London's Albert Hall in less than two hours. In a single week, the packaging thrown away by the British equals the weight of 245 jumbo jets. Since our enjoyment of what we buy seems to be short-lived, perhaps we could start by making a little more of what we're paying for. Then perhaps we could relax a little, safe in the knowledge that we've got something right, that we can stop chasing after the next new thing and the next, driven on by the insatiable desire for something better.

Dear Sloth

By now we all know who can give us the perfect insight into how it should be done, don't we? Let's hear it for the sloth.

Dear Sloth

I've never heard so much rubbish as all this talk about rubbish. What is it, after all, but another name for recycling? I think somebody once said there's nothing new under the sun, and he was right. There's nothing new in people grumbling about all this either. What about the Puritans – they tried to stop people having fun too. And the Communists – they were real eco-freaks in one way (give or take the odd nuclear reactor) because people couldn't waste what they didn't have in the first place, could they? But where did it leave them? As the biggest spenders on earth – bling, bling, bling, and loving every minute of it.

I'm just fed up with being told by some environmental lord god almighty that I must live my life in a way that keeps him (or her – mustn't forget the hers involved in all this nonsense, must we?) happy. If they want to deprive themselves, let them, but I work hard and want to enjoy the benefits I've earned.

Big Spender

Hey Big Spender,

This is normal. You are a sensitive soul who cares about what people think of you, and you also want to live in your own way. Look around you: don't you see a lot of people like you – all stressed out about something they are not planning to change? This is all about your human fixation on choice, isn't it? Shall I be this, or shall I be that, and whatever I choose will someone else like me? So exhausting. Do like a sloth – be what you are, and don't give a toss. It's all a load of recycling anyway.

Dear Sloth

I watched some old film footage on TV recently and was surprised at how happy and smart even the apparently poorer people looked. I've always been told that the world was dirty and miserable back in those days. I then walk down my local high street on a Saturday morning, look around me, and end up asking myself, 'How come people looked better than this when they had no money and nothing much to choose from?' The tide of lycra-clad, doughnut-shaped horrors that come lumbering towards me is quite scary. I wonder if there is an inverse relationship between money and taste. Britain is supposed to be one of the richest nations on earth; America is the richest, I believe; and we seem to have turned into the bad taste capitals of it. Is it totally unacceptable to think that the past may have had something on us — and is it now far too late for us to change?

Gobsmacked

Dear Gobsmacked

This is a normal development of excess — a sloth's worst nightmare (after harpy eagles, of course). We have a saying — I don't know if people have ever heard it — 'Waste not, want not', but I think what you are describing here is more a case of 'Waist not, want not'. Fat is a way to let the world know you've got more than them. Unfortunately, it doesn't allow for tailoring. But look around you: do you see really wealthy people looking like that? No. Your local high street inhabitants will eventually learn. In the meantime just don't stand below the tree when they start to offload.

Dear Sloth

I love travel but I don't want to be responsible for destroying the planet. I've heard about carbon footprints and they make sense to me. Do you agree with me that we should all be given a carbon allowance to spend as we choose, so if I save on things like car journeys I can fly off, guilt-free, on holiday? Or do you think there's no guilt-free way to travel? I'd really love your opinion, because I know how environmentally sound you and your species are, and I have to decide whether I can afford to book a flight to Greece or not, as I've already had one trip abroad this year.

Uncertain Traveller

Dear Uncertain Traveller

It is normal to confuse the two, but unfortunately, you are lumping us sloths in with the eco-extremists just because we know how to balance our lives. To deal with your question, however: ask yourself if 'go' means 'fly'. Sloths can and do fly (vertically and mostly downwards) but are not happy fliers. On the other hand, we just love to move through water – such a gentle, supportive way to travel if you have to cover distances. As you must know by now, I never give advice, but I wonder whether you might not consider making arrangements for a more leisurely extended trip across land and sea next year. Then you would feel so very virtuous and enjoy the more culturally complete immersion. If you have doubts about the benefits of water over flight, just look around you – which looks more relaxed, a bluebottle or a goldfish?

Dear Sloth

We don't want our little girl to grow up as a full-on consumer; in fact, we'd really be happier if she didn't watch any TV, as it's so full of adverts that brainwash kids to force their parents to buy things. But that would make her stand out when she starts school (she's three at the moment), and we want her to be as normal as possible. We know it's going to be difficult when she gets there anyway, as there will be kids all around her loaded with all the junk we don't want her to have. How can we hold out against buying all this rubbish without making her suffer?

Junk Junkers

Dear Junk Junkers

This is a normal part of modern life: wanting your kids to be better than other people's. There's nothing wrong with that. It's quite normal, in fact. Some people think it's to do with having more; others think it's to do with having less. But look around you – how many children who are their parents' social experiments turn out happily? Read Edmund Gosse's **Father and Son** (we sloths have long memories); his father wanted him to do without Christmas pudding – not a good idea, he hated his dad. We sloths always look down on sloths from other trees, but wouldn't dream of saying so. Don't make a stand over your family's superiority. Take it lying down.

And that's quite enough. Time to crawl on.

SLOTH HELPLINE NUMBER FIVE
– APPEARANCE

We are not crawling on very far, as it happens, since appearance is pretty much another consumer issue these days. In the past, what we looked like was the outcome, by and large, of what nature dictated, covered to varying degrees by what fashion dictated, topped off with some kind of hairdo, and a hat. All of which was read by our neighbours as a statement about who we were in terms of class (knight or knave), beliefs (church or chapel) and job (factory owner or farmer). We took our lead from our neighbours, they took their lead from us, and we all limited our ambitions to looking smarter, prettier, wealthier than those immediately around us.

As recently as the 1950s, young people's fashions were almost identical to their parents' and neighbours', with teenage girls cramming themselves into totally unnecessary roll-ons and putting their hair in curlers in order to look just like Mum, and boys, even in the heat of summer, going out in suits, ties and sports jackets, carbon copies of their dads. But since the explosion of the media into every area of our lives, our attention has been opened up to worldwide ways of doing things. Our appearance is now more likely to be influenced by magazine columns and the latest look sported by film stars and catwalk models than by our boring old families and neighbours.

Who shall I be?

Worldwide ways – worldwide options. No longer confined by the habits and opinions of the people around us, all of a sudden there are no limits – to image, to spending, to reality. It's all choice, choice, choice – who shall I be, what shall I be, what shall I look like? Why take the time to live the life when we can have it all in the look? Why train when with head to toe Nike we can be Beckham? We can be smart, sports casual, grunge, boho ... We can declare ourselves urban business powerhouse, country posh, wild and wacky, all without the need to change a single thing about ourselves except our wardrobe (which all the while is probably based in some unprepossessing suburb). What you see is no longer necessarily what you get. We all have the chance to re-invent ourselves now with the facility and speed of a Madonna, Posh and Becks, Kylie Minogue or Michael Jackson, give or take the quality of the cut and colour.

All of which goes some way to explaining why, though almost every household now has its own washing machine, we seem to need so many more clothes than ever before. We just can't get enough of clothes, of style, of choice.

The colour glossies are in large part responsible for this phenomenon. They inculcate in us a sense of inadequacy, while at the same time selling advertising space to the purveyors of the goods specifically designed to help us feel adequate again (until next month). Clever, isn't it? These magazines give us the really hard sell on how we should aim to look as good as people who spend all their waking hours – and many hundreds of thousands of pounds – on looking perfect.

Once again we are caught in the modern bind that we are doomed to fail by comparison with perfection. But because we have become sold on the consumerist ideal that we really can buy our way into or out of anything, and that we will have failed in our duty as model modern citizens if we fail to be as good-looking as the best, we are willing to suspend our disbelief. So we go out and buy yet another set of clothes that we are certain will make us look as good as, well, whichever supermodel looks that good in them – despite the fact we are a head shorter than them, 20 years older and somewhat overweight.

None of this endless triumph of hope over expectation comes exactly cheap, of course, but that doesn't stop us giving away vast quantities of what we've bought almost immediately to charity shops. Sales worth about £1,570 million are made annually in British charity shops, which suggests that the pursuit of an inadvisable image will cost many of us a pretty penny in the course of a lifetime. One lucky charity-shopper I know of, recently picked up a pair of brand-new designer boots (label still attached) worth £400 for the bargain price of £20. Great for her, and great for the charity, but what does this say about the state of mind of the person who gave them away? Or about the state of their body image if they were confused about what suited them to the tune of a cool £400?

Not all the gods cracked us up to be

This leads us to the subject of distorted body image, or body dysmorphia. At its most extreme, this condition leads the sufferer to have serious delusions about their bodies (and sometimes their boots), which may include believing that body parts either don't belong to them or are deformed in dreadful ways. This might sound bizarre but slightly amusing if it hadn't led to a number of these sadly deluded people actually having arms and legs surgically removed. Extraordinary perhaps, but at some time or other, even if only when we were image-conscious adolescents, most of us have experienced a miniature version of the same type of delusion, regarding our nose as too big, or our hair too fine, or our appendage too small to be exposed in public without embarrassment. (Raquel Welch reportedly even believed that having hairs on her toes constituted a trichological crime against humanity.)

But now it's not only the mentally disturbed and teenagers (for whom, let's face it, mental disturbance is practically the norm) who are likely to have a distorted sense of what they look like. More and more people feel at odds with their shape these days, and, sadly, this phenomenon is being seen in younger and younger children. A study by Sussex University, England, recently claimed that children as young as *six* were left feeling unhappy with their, perfectly normal and healthy, body shape after being shown pictures of Barbie, the hugely successful but impossibly skinny fashion doll. According to Helga Dittmar, the psychologist who carried out the study, 'These ultra-thin images not only lowered young girls' body esteem but also decreased their satisfaction with their actual body size, making them desire a thinner body.' She added that this insecurity about body shape could lead to eating disorders in later life.

Anorexia nervosa, which affects over a million people in the UK alone, is one of the most common eating disorders, and the incidence is still on the rise amongst teenagers, presumably because they are increasingly exposed to the marketing of 'perfection'. But it's not only teenagers who fall prey to the pressure to be thin; children are now presenting with anorexia at earlier and earlier ages. Indeed, the prevalence of eating disorders is increasing across all age groups and both sexes. Again, research suggests that this is due, in the main, to the increased pressure to conform to a single, gender-specific – and for most of us highly unrealistic – body shape.

Bodies – how did we humans ever fall for the idea that there could be such a thing as a perfect standard model? There are about 6,515,793,569 people in the world; why do so many of us in the West want to look like a particular hundred of them? The pressure to conform to the ideal, simply makes 99.9 per cent of the Western population feel dysmorphic.

This leads us back to unnecessary surgery. The pressure to look like a fashion doll has resulted in an upsurge in cosmetic surgery. Like eating disorders, cosmetic surgery is becoming a phenomenon among younger and younger people. In the USA, 331,000 cosmetic surgery procedures are carried out on under-eighteens every year. In the UK, it was recently reported that a girl of 16 had had a boob job, with her mother's proud support and before she was even fully grown. Let's not wait for nature – that old laggard – to take its course. We can turn ourselves into whatever we want to be, whenever we want to be it, as long as we can afford the surgeon's fee.

Not even the glaring evidence of the (still just about) walking, talking Michael Jackson has been enough to dissuade people from the belief that any one of us can achieve some standardised Barbie-doll version of 'perfection' – witness the popularity of the recent rash of body makeover programmes that have descended onto our credulous heads. These programmes suggest that no matter what damage we've willingly done to ourselves in the past (be it the elephant skin produced by years of sunbathing, the teeth stained brown by our 20-a-day nicotine intake, or the boil-in-the bag bottom left over from years of yo-yo dieting), it's never too late to achieve a brand new body. A branded new body, in fact, one that comes with the programme's logo, and by which we will ever after be known – 'Oh, there goes John with his new *Chump to a Champ* muscleman body.' It's a body designed and achieved by any one of a number of identikit, frigidly feline presenters and a panel of well-paid experts.

The business of conforming to one universal standard of perfection is a modern tyranny. Time was, every area had its own beauties and its own standards, just as it had its own shops, its own foods and its own tastes in everything. Some of those beauties would even be famous through generations, 'the lovely Countess of Colchester', 'your Great-aunt Rosie, whose eyes inspired poets', 'Mary Mitchell, whose lips were famed far and wide'. Admired then, but by comparison with Claudia Schiffer or Angelina Jolie, how would they fare today? A hundred years ago, most country girls and boys would probably compare themselves with no more than 100 people in their lifetime and could claim their place in Little Snodbury's Miss World or Mr Universe line-up. Today, most children in the developed world have to compare themselves with the best that five continents (I'm not sure about Antarctica) can come up with. No wonder we're all so dissatisfied.

A little dab of powder

Given that most of us simply *are* going to try to improve on nature, what lengths is it actually worth going to in the name of physical perfection? At the end of the day, when we see the 'new improved' versions of the men and women who've gone under the knife for our entertainment, do they really look younger because of all the expensive, painful surgery they've had, or simply because they've acquired a trimmer figure, a more stylish wardrobe, a good hair cut and a lot of well-applied slap? I'm sure many of us will have come across someone who's spent a fortune on a wonderfully Botoxed face but is still better known for being lardy. You have to wonder if we're not a little confused about what we're trying to achieve.

The fact is that if we were genuinely looking simply to improve our appearance, a small sum spent in the makeup department of our local chemist, a quick trim of our topknot, and a trip to a charity shop might do as much for the majority of us as any of those surgical procedures when worn 'naked' – and we'd get the whole thing done cheaply and painlessly in less than half a day. But we're not looking simply to improve our appearance, are we? We're actually on a never-ending quest for an impossible ideal. What we desire is never to be satisfied. At 50 we think we'd be happy with the skin of a 20-year-old, but if that's true, why weren't we happy at 20?

The truth is we don't know what we really want, unless it's whatever we don't have at the moment, whether that's to be young, smooth, thin and sleek, or just much more like Catherine Zeta Jones. Anyway, 93 per cent of the UK population manage to spend £5 billion a year on cosmetics and toiletries that '*may* effect a slight to modest improvement in wrinkles'. That's an awful lot to spend on a '*may*'.

Years ago we *knew* what we wanted. We wanted to look good as who we were, doing what we did. Now, taking our lead from models and superstars, we want to look good as it's humanly possible to look. We want to look as if we are sexpots, business tycoons, surf dudes, fey gossamer dreamers, yummy mummies, caring daddies, romantic smackheads, glossy Hollywood stars, eco warriors, footballers' wives and/or whatever else is the look of the moment.

Dear Sloth

So let's see what solutions our sloth has to offer.

Dear Sloth

I'm an attractive young woman, according to my friends anyway, but I'm just not particularly interesting to look at. I suppose I'm average – blondish hair, medium height, slim, even features, good legs. I have reasonable dress sense but tend to wear rather a lot of sensible clothes, as I travel to work by train and bus and do quite a bit of sport at weekends. I don't have a boyfriend at the moment but have been asked to several summer do's and hope to be lucky. The big thing is I want to make more impact. I want to stand out from the crowd and attract everyone's attention when I walk into a room. I don't want to do bling but I do want to do zing. How do I go about it?

Dull

Dear Dull

You sound very normal. How lovely. But you want to be abnormal; that's normal, too – most people seem to want this. Most celebrities spend the first half of their life wanting to be noticed and the second wanting not to be noticed. This is where choice falls down: you can't be noticed just when it suits you. We sloths know this. It's is how we've survived so very long – by not being any more noticeable than we can possibly help. Look around you: how many sloths can you see? Precisely. We keep a very low profile, with our lovely, natural, blend-in-with-the-greenery outfit, and that's why we don't attract predators (apart from those accursed harpy eagles).

On the other hand, if you don't mind becoming prey to all and sundry, then I suggest wearing whatever doesn't suit the background. So, if you're going to Ascot, wear a spangly top and lycra leggings; for a country wedding, skinny jeans and bright shiny trainers; for a weekend in the country, pack a selection of halter-necks and little white shorts. I think I can guarantee you'll be outstanding in all of these – and not a touch of bling in sight.

But if you'd rather not ... you sound very lovely as you are, so why not just do your best to feel comfortable with how you are or, failing that, think of taking one of your least attractive friends around with you?

Dear Sloth

As a rather 'cuddly' person I take exception to some of the comments in the helpline on appearance. It contains rather a lot of hypocrisy on the subject of weight. One minute you say there's an unacceptable level of fascism about fat (a stance with which I happen to agree); the next you are banging on about people being lardy. So where exactly do you stand? I would quite like to know as, in point of fact, I have been giving the matter of shifting the odd pound or two a little consideration, as the doctor seems to think it advisable for blood pressure reasons or some such nonsense. Also, are you in any position to be talking about weight issues? You don't look too skinny yourself.

Cuddly

Dear Cuddly

Hmmm. It's normal for those with an issue to be defensive, which is why you will not find me so. Sloths are never plump. Neither are we sensitive to hurts, which means we can take the good out of what might seem toxic to others. People might find it useful to adapt in similar ways, especially on the subject of weight, which I gather can be quite a tricky one. Fail to take the bull by the horns and tell someone they are in danger of becoming a bit of a porker when they are young and you condemn them to a lifetime of diets and fat – not a lot of fun, just look around you. Embarrass them briefly and you save them a lot of problems. It's just a whole lot easier not to have to make the effort to improve yourself after the event. So we sloths try to keep life simple by remaining as perfect as the day we were born. An occasional long swim, a good green diet, no fats and of course no drink (is your face a little bit pink by any chance?), and we enjoy extremely low blood pressure as well as extraordinarily good looks. And no excess. You should try it.

Sloth helplines

Dear Sloth

Please can you help? I spend hours in front of the bathroom mirror looking at everything that's wrong with me. My mother bangs on the door from time to time asking if I'm all right. She thinks I've got constipation. I can't tell her I think I'm turning into a freak, can I? I'm sure I am though. How can I ever get a girlfriend looking the way I do: freaky nose, freaky hair, freaky sunken chest and freaky – well, you know what. I want to be normal, like other boys at school, like Shayne Smith, for example. What can I do?

Kevin Jones, a freak (aged 13)

Dear Kevin Jones

You are perfectly normal, not that you will ever believe me, at least until you're 35, which is also normal. You will also not believe me when I say: look around you, nearly everyone else looks just like you. Even Shayne Smith, who admittedly is as good as it gets on the average high street (and let's hope you're not aiming any higher), is hardly any happier with how he looks. But you won't believe that either. So there are only two things left for you to do ... No, there are only three things left for you to do. These are:

1 Hide yourself away for ever.

2 Hide the mirror away for ever – or at least for five years. Mirrors are a menace. We sloths have lived without them for thousands of years in absolute contentment, and in the absolute belief that we are beautiful. We have no way of comparing ourselves with anyone.

3 Smile. Everyone who smiles is very beautiful and well liked by girls (or boys, depending, or both – who cares?)

Having done one, or possibly two, of these things, you should find your life a little easier, though not too easy I hope – you are 13, after all.

Dear Sloth

I'm 55 going on 15. I like to wear exciting clothes, put on makeup and party with the best of them. I enjoy experimenting with different looks and hair-dos – I've recently ditched short skirts in favour of a gypsy look. I spend quite large sums on my appearance and admit to being a bit of a sucker at times for the latest facial technology. My friends say it's time to slow down and tone down. Do you think I should take any notice or carry on as I am?

Baby Boomer

Dear Baby Boomer

This dilemma is normal for Baby Boomers – look around you. The big question is who are you doing it for? If you're doing it to impress other people of your own age, the most you can ever hope for is that you don't offend (which is why we sloths groom regularly but don't try to outdo each other in looks). When someone looks better than you, it's simply irritating. (If they look a whole lot worse, it's simply unpleasant.) To younger people, the most you can ever hope to be is someone who looks okay for their age – think Madonna, and look at the money and time she spends. To old people, you'll always just look blurred. If, on the other hand, you think you're doing it for yourself, the real questions are: why are you making such an effort and do you feel comfortable inside the end result? If you don't, you're not being totally honest with yourself about your motivation. A sloth avoids pointless effort and always tries to feel comfortable – it's the only way to enjoy life.

When we're agonising over which boots to buy, wondering whether we've put on too much weight to be attractive to a hippo, considering plastic surgery on our totally inoffensive nose or splashing out on the latest must-have Lazarus dermopeptoglobwelox skin rebirthing product of the day, perhaps we should bear in mind what Hamlet said to Horatio about cosmetics as he played with Yorick's decaying skull:

> Now get you to my lady's chamber, and tell her, let her paint an inch thick, to this favour she must come.

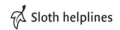

SLOTH HELPLINE NUMBER SIX
– WORK AND AMBITION

The old conundrum, do we live to work or work to live?, seems to have been answered for a large proportion of the working population today. After travelling to work, putting in our eight hours and travelling back, we don't have time to do much else apart from sleep, so the answer is we live to work. There are so many of us opting for the same commute route through life nowadays that for six months of the year we are more likely to spend sunrise and sunset on the road or in a train than in our own homes. The British spend, on average, 45 minutes a day travelling to work, twice as long as people in more laid-back Italy. For some committed (or mad, take your pick) Brits, the journey time can be as long as *four hours*. Which, if you dared to do the maths, would add up to a whole five weeks in a year. Forget sunrise and sunset, these people are lucky to be home much before midnight.

Seven out of ten British people living outside the London area do their commuting by car, and they travel 17 per cent further in their cars than 10 years ago. Despite that fact, when asked by the RAC what they would do if their journey time doubled, most drivers said they wouldn't consider changing the way they travelled, moving house or finding a new job. They said they'd simply set out earlier and leave more time for the journey. And for this entertaining way of spending our time – sitting nose-to-tail in a traffic jam (or in a packed train) – some of us are prepared to pay out one-third of our salary. We must love our work. Or so any rational sloth would think.

Down with work

The British reportedly work longer hours than those living in any other European country. So why, oh why, do two-thirds of British workers say that they are unhappy at work? And why do they take 6.5 million days off a year explicitly due to stress and depression? It doesn't seem to make any sense at all. Perhaps it's just that a very small number of people never bother actually going home at all.

It appears, however, that it's not the length of the working day that's an issue so much as the people we work with. Yes, our colleagues are the flies in the ointment. Indeed, according to the head of administration at a large college in the south-west of England, who I spoke to recently, the main problem she has to face is people. As she herself put it, but for the annoying (actually she used a rather more spicy word) staff and students the whole place would run beautifully. And she's not exactly out on her own misanthropic limb, because apparently 47 per cent of senior managers in the UK have no problem with the pay and conditions of their posts, and would find all their responsibilities absolutely fine if only they didn't have to manage all those pesky people (leaving the managers to do what, precisely?). Not that the pesky people get on any better with each other either, though. According to the business website management-issues.com, British offices are characterised by rude and aggressive behaviour, ranging from copying people in unnecessarily on e-mails criticising others to ignoring junior staff in meetings.

So it rather looks as if it's all our own fault. We *do* do work it seems; it's just that we don't do people. Perhaps we could do with learning a bit about happy co-existence from the sloth.

That, of course, would involve letting go of our need to compete with each other all the time, which it seems we are hardly likely to do, considering that competition is a large part of the reason humans go to work in the first place these days. We just love to get ahead, to whizz our way up the corporate ladder, to maximise our potential, to reach the pinnacle of our profession, to win the glittering prizes. How many people nowadays say that they want a steady job and a slow progression up the ladder, but if promotion wasn't to happen they'd be perfectly happy just to stay put? Never mind all the media talk about school children suffering because they have no access to competitive sports any more, once they get to work they're going to be overwhelmed by the yells of, 'All's fair in love, war and work, and the losers buy the drinks.' The truth is, we are constantly encouraged to compete. How else do you account for the making and success of the internationally syndicated TV programme *The Apprentice*, in which people compete – fiercely – for a job with a top company?

As the contestants in *The Apprentice* know, there can only ever be one winner, which means that there are always going to be many losers. And as nobody ever suggested, at school or in the business books, that failure was an option, it makes us a little bit cross when it arrives. It makes the younger ones among us especially cross, it appears. According to a Gallup poll in the UK, 18–30-year-olds are four times more likely to feel angry about frustrations at work than are people over 50. Once again, according to the poll, these frustrations come down to the irritating people they have to work with.

Work for work's sake

So we get up at dawn to flog our way to work through the heaving traffic and bad weather. We arrive all raring to go, panting to discover our strengths, fulfil our potential and win the corporate prize, but then we discover there's something nasty in the woodshed. Or maybe more than one thing. We don't like the people, especially when they beat us to the prize – that's pretty clear; but what about the job itself? Surely we like that.

Well, perhaps we can take five, before we have to nip out to the Transpeople Diversity and Equal Rights Awareness training day, to ask ourselves what we really do get, once we've arrived at work, from the endless round of filling in questionnaires about how many key performance targets have been fulfilled; reading equal opportunities legislation; ticking boxes; and writing reports in triplicate about how many of us took turns to hold the holder while someone else, trained in hygiene, health and safety, replaced the loo roll in the occupational health facility? Then, when we've thought about it, we might quite possibly find that even though we adore the intellectual challenges of all the above, actually quite a lot of the time we're at work we're not really working at the job itself at all, not in the way a ploughman used to work, or a plasterer still does, carrying out the task named in the job description. We might find we're not exactly doing what it says on the tin, because for so much of the time we're too busy creating the framework of our work and being the facilitators of our working time.

Never mind, once we've managed to get on top of the awareness days and the directives for an hour or two and done a bit of the job itself, we may discover that we actually find it quite boring ... and then realise that we'll never get promotion out of it because there's a right old git who's got it in for us and has undermined our position with the boss (sorry, line manager).

So we'll never make it to the top, but we can always go to a business guru to get advice on how to find ourselves a more fulfilling job. The following, rather sensible, gems of wisdom are offered by business guru Rob Yeung:

- Know what you want to do: go for the most likes and fewest dislikes.
- Do you have the right skills? Think about those you might have to acquire. Seek other people's views of your strengths and weaknesses.

- Plan what steps to take. Think of the barriers and how to overcome them.

- Often your career goals will depend on others. Learn how to influence them – people give opportunities to those they like best.

- Boost your skills. Work with other teams. If you have been in the same role for two or three years, get a transfer to another department or a secondment. Failing that, get involved in a project outside your department.

- Accepting change – and helping others through it – will make your career take off. Experience of change will make your CV shine.

- Think of at least two ways to solve any problem.

- Network: meet lots of people interested in mutual gain.

- Know how headhunters work. Raise your profile to attract their attention.

- Don't let the thrill of a job offer go to your head. A few days' reflection can save years of grief in the wrong job.

Yes, you could probably have worked most of that out for yourself, but there's nothing to knock in any of it – if what you want is a career. But what has that actually got to do with a *job*?

Chippendale again

We're back to Chippendale's *Directory* again. The advice given by nearly all modern business gurus is more about design than about manufacture or function. They've got nothing to say about how we can become better at what we do, because they know pretty much nothing about it. Imagine Bill Gates ever having needed that kind of help – or indeed the craftsmen of the past. They worked really hard to develop their skills, but once they'd got them they didn't constantly try to redefine them or make them fit a whole new set of parameters. A blacksmith knew about horses, fire and the properties of iron, and he knew about them for life. A blacksmith was a blacksmith, was a blacksmith. It was what he did and who he was.

But that all changed somewhere near the end of the twentieth century, when we were all told that sticking with one job for a lifetime was old hat. We could be whatever we wanted, and we could be it whenever we wanted. Unfortunately, what a large number of people seemed to want to be was film directors, actors and singing stars, which is why a large number of former film and media studies students are now working in MacDonalds. Not to worry, though, because we always have the option of re-inventing ourselves any number of times. A spell as a gastronomic advisor will be great for facilitating a sideways move into another career.

Change is now endemic at work, the reason being the modern myth that growth = improvement = success. It's all change for change's sake, but somehow we allow ourselves to be persuaded that change will actually keep our own career rolling. It's all change or else ... 'What?', why don't we all shout? 'Might we actually learn how to do something properly?'

In one of the most famous business books on the sacred subject of change (possibly because it has one of the silliest titles), *Who Moved My Cheese*, author Dr Spencer Johnson has handily printed on a wedge of cheese the motivating, but rather doom-laden, pronouncement, 'If You Do Not Change, You Can Become Extinct' – to which the sloth would almost certainly reply, 'Yes, But Only Very, Very Slowly.' In which time the sloth might also have had a life.

As for the rest of us, we buzz around, chasing after change even while we haven't got to grips with all the demands of our current working situation. Faxes fly, meetings proliferate and e-mails multiply like locusts. Always behind ourselves, perhaps we should consider slowing things down a bit. The pace has obviously been a bit too fast for us.

Dear Sloth

Now for the sloth's take on human ambition and attitudes at work.

Dear Sloth

I am a victim of bullying in the workplace. I have been in my department for ten years and never had real problems with any of my previous managers (and there were 12 of them), but since the latest one arrived two years ago, my life has been made hell. I'm very stressed, but I hardly dare take sick leave – even though I know I'm entitled to more leave than I've taken this year – because I know she'll make an issue of it again. Last year I had a very worrying time at home and felt I couldn't cope, so the doctor signed me off for six weeks, and my manager made very unpleasant comments on my return, including the suggestion that I might need retraining for the job as I could be what she called de-skilled. She also had my desk moved, so that now I have to walk further to the photocopier and coffee machine. I've been told this is tantamount to intimidation and that I may have a case against her. What shall I do? If I take action I'll find it difficult to work in the same office as her, but if I don't, I think her bullying tactics will make me ill again.

Victim

Dear Victim

This is normal. You are now (for the first time) working for a humourless, target-driven obsessive. Look around you: they are everywhere these days. She expects people to work, work, work, and, as you can imagine, that does not go down well with a sloth. However there are a few considerations you may not have thought about:

- If you win your case – and who could doubt that the action with your desk was anything less than vengeful – you may also find yourself promoted. Will you want all that extra work and responsibility?

- If the company does not sack your manager, they may insist you all go on a team-building weekend together. How do you feel about paintballing and walking on burning coals?

- We sloths are very pragmatic. Since you're taking less time off work than ever before, it sounds as though your health is on the mend. Perhaps you can take the good from that and learn to live with your bitch of a manager

Dear Sloth

I don't live to work, I work to live. I've got thousand of pounds of student debt, which I feel I'm going to be spending the rest of my life paying off, and I have a vague idea that one day I might like to buy a house with my girlfriend and get married and all that stuff. I had dreams once that I might make something of myself – you know have my own business, that kind of thing – so that I could actually do what I've been trained to do. I spent four years at uni doing a fine arts degree – hoping to produce limited edition china – and what did I get out of it? £20,000 of debt and a boring job in an insurance assessor's firm. It's miles from where I live and I spend half my salary just getting there. I expect you remember times when people just thought, sod that for a lark and went off to live in a commune. Were they fun?

Hopeless

Dear Hopeless

You don't like being a drone. This is normal. As is believing that living in a rambling unheated old house with a crowd of similarly deluded, dope-smoking acquaintances is fun. Now I imagine it surprises you to hear this coming from a sloth, but let me tell you that people have been trying that one for years and it's never worked, not even for mad Romantic poets, so what chance is there for people who've been used to hot water and a bath of their own? Despite what others might assume, we sloths do not approve of such a way of life. The press gets us wrong. We are not a lazy mess; we're simply unwilling to overexert ourselves and not given to unnecessary vanity.

But I think what you're really asking is if I can give you any advice on how to get meaning out of your life, and of course the answer is no. I don't do advice. What would be the point? Look around you: do people ever take good advice? All I will say is that I sympathise (and that's unusual for a sloth). It must be hard being a work slave, looking forward to 10 years without let up, in the cold realistic light of the dawn of the twenty-first century – almost as bad as being in the same position 100 years ago. We sloths also have to forage for our daily bread, but we just get on with it without all the existentialist angst. Why don't you chill out and try it?

Dear Sloth

I have a friend who is always complaining about her working conditions and expecting this and expecting that. If she snags her tights on the office desk, she virtually expects them to be replaced. She gets taken out to lunches and given weekend breaks as bonuses, but complains she has to dress up for do's. She's forever going on about how she would like to have my job. I'm so lucky, apparently, because I get to work from home at a really interesting job and have all that time to lie in bed in the mornings while she's having to struggle in to work. I am a self-employed journalist, get intermittent work and have a mortgage, and I want to strangle her (nicely). What do you suggest I do to make her SHUT THE **** UP?

Irritated

Dear Irritated

It's normal for people to think the other man's (or woman's) grass is always greener. Sloths can't get their heads around this, as they don't spend their time pondering what else, where else and how else they might be living their lives. They just live their lives and make the most of them.

Eating is a fine thing to be doing, sleeping is a fine thing to be doing, relaxing is a fine thing to be doing, swimming ... You get the message. But wondering about alternatives – when you are not going to try them out – why? Look around you: how many lives are wasted in wondering? So, perhaps you could do your friend a favour by offering her the chance to live out her dream. You're a journalist, sell the idea. Swap lives and have the alternative in reality – reality TV even. Your friend should like that. But tell her there's one stipulation: she must actually live on the money she earns by her efforts as a journalist, and you get to live on her salary. I think that should do the trick.

Dear Sloth

I've just got a brilliant new job, and I'm thrilled. I feel so lucky. I came straight out of college and fell into it at a careers seminar, so I've not had to struggle to find work at all. My friends are all so envious – in the nicest possible way. It is all even better when I get into the office, which is in a beautiful new all-glass building in the London Docklands, and I've been given a desk overlooking the river, with a new computer and a laptop, too, and been told to ask for anything else I think I'll need. The loos are unbelievable, all limestone basins, suede and marble, with orchids in every cubicle, and we have endless fresh coffee and Italian biscuits. I can't think of anything else I could possibly want. Everyone I work with is just so nice to me. They're a brilliant crowd. I have a wonderful line manager, who has already offered me any amount of training opportunities, including a personality enhancement weekend at a spa resort in Wales, and a team-building white water rafting week in Brittany. It's all beyond my dreams, so I expect you're wondering what I can possibly have to write to you about? It's very strange. I expect I'm being stupid or something and it is all really absolutely obvious, but I don't like to ask. The fact is, I have no idea what goes on here, what the business is, or what anyone wants me to do. Have you ever come across a situation like this before?

Spooked

Dear Spooked

I would like to put your mind at rest; this is normal. As you say, this is your first job and you have had no experience of looking for work before. If you had, you would know that the same mystery exists everywhere. Try not to feel spooked. Look around you, does anybody else have the slightest idea of what the company's about? After all it's not a tailor's, is it? You are now in the corporate zone. You are not a name, you are a career.

As everybody knows, I do not offer advice, but perhaps you might find some of the following ideas worth chewing over for a year or two:

1 Some people have a natural desire to keep track of their own products (something a sloth understands). If you are one of them, consider whether you might prefer to work in more direct contact with the products you are trying to sell.

2 Sloths do not believe in unnecessary stress. You could accept your good luck while it lasts, and be adaptable when it runs out. There are a lot of London loos still needing to be filled with orchids (see point no. 1).

3 Sloths do believe in camouflage – as, it would appear, do your work colleagues. Go with the flow, learn the corporate lingo, do the courses, take the promotions. Do sloths ask where trees come from?

And on that eminently sensible bit of business advice it's time to move on to …

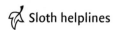

Sloth helpline number seven
– causes and caring, worry and blame

These two findings about modern life were recently printed side by side on one page of a weekend newspaper:

1. Living in a flat is bad for our health. People who live in flats have twice the risk of injury and six times the risk of poisoning as people living in any other kind of home, according the Professor of Public Health at the University of Wales.

2. Scheduled sex (very 'now' in our busy, busy society) can cause ruinous performance anxiety, according to the National University of Singapore. A clinical sexologist(!) adds, 'The more a man thinks about it, the smaller his penis becomes.'

This frankly bizarre combination goes to show that modern life is a dangerous and anxiety-producing business. Or, alternatively (again according to an expert, but one who comes from a slightly different field), 'There is nothing either good or bad, but thinking makes it so.'

And it does rather seem that we are thinking ourselves into a bit of a state.

As soon as we've allowed ourselves to be, well, sort of, convinced that MMR jabs don't lead to autism, that millions of us are not about to go all wobbly with CJD, that mobile phones may not immediately fry the brains of our little darlings (whatever else they may do to them), that one dead swan does not a pandemic make ... we start looking for other things to think ourselves into a panic about. What about recycling? Perhaps that's good for two things: first to beat ourselves up over because we need to do more of it; and then to beat ourselves up over because draconian councils fine people for not doing it properly and perhaps we are turning into a police state. Then there are all the other problems to do with the environment to worry about ... and all the other signs of a police state. Perhaps we should be building enough new low-cost housing for those who can't afford to buy a place to live. Of course, in the name of social inclusivity we should, but if we do, what about the flood plains and the lesser spotted goshawks? Why not build on brown field sites instead, an obvious choice and one that will bring money to areas in need of growth ... But hang on a minute, what will happen to the bugs? Bugs are essential to the existence of the eco-structure of the entire universe. If we kill them off on the brown field sites ...! Why not up the eco-scare ante? Why not up any ante, in fact, because each new minority interest group scare will bring on our favourite people, the experts, to tell us that we'd better start to worry about this one, because if we don't ... we'll probably offend someone.

And that is fast becoming the worst offence of all. We need only think of Prince Harry doing what post-war party-goers did for years by dressing up in an *Allo Allo*-style Nazi uniform and then look at the offence he caused. And that's something else we really should be worrying about. But not too much, just in case it makes us stressed. And we all know we should be worried about rising levels of stress.

Trying to be too perfect

Is it because we see so many film sets that we think the world should be perfect? Or is it because we hear so many politicians setting it all to rights? Whatever the reason, we do seem to be convinced that, even if the earth and its population aren't currently perfect, they are, all the same, perfectly perfectible. We must be convinced of this, otherwise we would surely realise that trying to eliminate risk, outlaw offence, make rules to offset ill health, and set up institutional Aunt Sally's to take the blame in place of God a) will never work, and b) will make for an awful lot of unnecessary effort and stress.

Putting a label on a chainsaw telling the user not to attempt to stop the moving blade with their hand, or a warning on a bottle of sleeping pills suggesting that swallowing one may result in drowsiness, doesn't result in safety and never will until the user is also forced, by law, to read the instructions. Not that the manufacturers are interested whether we do or not; what they're interested in is avoiding blame. If they can show they've done their bit, who cares that we, the consumer, have lost a finger in an idiotic accident or can't sleep for irritation. Who cares whether we can even access and enjoy the product. All that matters is that we can't sue them – yet. You can be sure that the lawyers will eventually find a way; after all, according to the UK Institute of Actuaries, the compensation culture is worth about £10 billion a year. More litigation: won't that make us feel better?

Things to worry about squat in the corners of our minds like toxic toads, just waiting to leap out and startle us whenever we begin to relax and let our guard down. And once we've spotted them squatting there, it takes an extraordinary effort to ignore them. It's plain hard work wondering if we've just offended someone by a casual reference to Napoleon having been a very little man. It's plain hard work rewriting language so that 'mortal' becomes 'life-limiting' and 'indoctrinating' becomes 'assisting people with their knowledge'. It's plain hard work wondering if exposure to sunlight will lead to cancer more quickly than non-exposure will lead to rickets. It's plain hard work worrying whether we're stunting our kids by under-intervention in their lives or swamping them by over-intervention. It's plain hard work trying diet after diet, worrying about whether unsaturated fats and high glycaemic indexes will eventually lead to compensatory overeating. It's plain hard work wondering if we'll be seen as slave traders if we're not concerned enough about third world debt. It's plain hard work sidestepping chuggers (charity muggers – those people lurking on the street anxious to persuade you to sign away a small monthly sum to a good cause) and making excuses to tearful friends collecting to save human life, flora and fauna in a place we've never heard of. It's plain hard work feeling that the only thing we can be intolerant of is intolerance itself.

Worrying too much is an effort. Searching desperately to find someone else to blame for every little thing that goes wrong is an effort. 'Caring' about every good cause that is brought to our attention is an effort. Being sensitive to every little hidden assault by life is an effort. All these things keep problems eternally in our minds, alive and kicking. Take the example of the woman seeking a divorce who was encouraged by her friends to take her husband for half his business, even though he'd made her a reasonable offer and she was finding the whole thing very stressful. But they persuaded her to keep on pushing, partly because it was a woman's right, partly because she was the wronged party, and largely because he was the one to blame. She finally made the whole messy business completely irrelevant by having a massive stroke and dying.

If we don't learn to tolerate intolerance (and a whole load of other things) fairly soon, even more of us are going to fall prey to stress in similar ways. Stuff, as somebody once said, happens, even to the best protected among us. Who could have failed to enjoy the teensiest bit of *Schadenfreude* on reading the following report in *The Times* recently,

> A group of health and safety officers were rescued by firefighters yesterday after the floor of their office collapsed during a discussion about safety procedures. The 21 officials who attended the first-floor meeting made a swift but unintentional descent to the ground floor accompanied by a conference table.

We simply can't make everything in the world work as we would like it to, however much we legislate, 'care' and worry about it all.

Future imperfect

If watching too much of life through film and TV screens really does result in so many of us believing in the perfectibility of life, then perhaps we should think about the city of Bath, in the south-west of England. It's a beautiful city and one that film and TV producers love to use as the backdrop to historical dramas. The trouble is, they always get the look of it wrong. They want a perfect Georgian or Regency scene, so they film the place as it is now, minus the cars and yellow lines. What we see is a tourist honey-pot without the tourists. What we should see is an ongoing, noisy, building site. And it never did get finished in the way that it was planned. War, death and bankruptcy got in the way of perfecting perfection.

Life's a messy, unfinished business, and it's one thing to want to improve it, but quite another to expect to perfect it.

After all, if we want to do like a sloth, we have to think like a sloth (give or take the desire for upside-down sex). Sloths don't worry, but they do deal with what's in front of them, even if it's a bit tough. Sloths don't try to perfect or over-control the planet, but they do adapt themselves to their environment. Sloths don't aim for the stars, but they do enjoy the heights when they are there – and shake it off when they fall.

You can't help feeling that they'd make a mound of compost out of much of our current legislation. Still, it's probably better to let the sloth speak for itself.

Dear Sloth

And now on to our final selection of sloth wisdom.

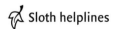

Dear Sloth

Is it just me, or does nothing work properly any more? I seem to spend half my life complaining about things – that's the half of my life that I'm not spending hanging on the phone, waiting to talk to an actual person to whom I can complain.

Nothing ever does what I expect it to do. The other day, I bought a new computer, expecting it to have all the latest programmes, only to get it home and find it had only basic ones as standard. Now I discover I have to pay extra for the ones I want. The company accepts no responsibility and says it should have been obvious that the latest software would come as extra and that I didn't ask the right questions. They made me feel like a fool – and left me wondering if I have cause for complaint about their attitude as well as their misleading advertising. I don't suppose I'll get any joy from them, but do you think I should get advice from a solicitor (I think you get half an hour free), or even approach a consumer advice TV programme about what must be a common problem?

Aggrieved

Dear Aggrieved

This is normal. Were you ever a child? Did the Painting by Numbers you produced ever look like the scene on the box? Did the electrical gizmo ever come complete with batteries? Did your Blue Peter Christmas mobile ever look better than a coat hanger with inadequate baubles?

I thought not. Look around you: do many things do all that they suggest to your imagination? Is anything other than Disneyland or a Honda Accord ever completely reliable? And if you'd never had the benefit of seeing consumer programmes such as Watchdog, might you now harbour the tiniest suspicion that you've been a bit of a twit? Sloths have a saying, 'The more things you have, the more worries you have.' As you know, I never give advice, so I'll just ask you a couple more questions and then it's over to you:

1 How long do you think it will take you to get through to Watchdog on the phone?

2 How long will it take you to earn the money to buy the extra computer programs you say you need?

3 Do you need them?

4 Have you ever heard of Jarndyce v Jarndyce or loss leaders?

And, lastly, have you thought of Googling sloths on your new computer? You might find that your most relaxing option yet.

Dear Sloth

Don't you think we live in the most selfish society imaginable? Me and some of my friends can't believe how obsessed by money and possessions some of our other friends are. They don't seem to care about anything but clubbing and clothes. They're so shallow. We really want our lives to make a difference to other people. I can't stand all the poverty and prejudice in the world. If it weren't for what we'd done to it, the rest of the world wouldn't have so many problems now, but some people just don't seem to care. I care so much, sometimes it hurts. I want to go somewhere deprived – a Third World country – so I can really make a difference. Where do you suggest and what do you think would be the best thing for me to do to make a real difference?

Distressed (age 15)

Dear Distressed

This is normal. At 15 you either want to waste yourself or rescue others. And then you want to sleep it off (the healthiest part of either, quite frankly). Hurting when you're an adolescent is normal, too, even for sloths. Take the last foot off Mum and sometimes you take a tumble. But then we sloths try to climb right back up. Sometimes you have to live with hurt; it happens. It won't do you any harm (unless there's a harpy eagle involved), but it sure as anything won't do anyone else any good.

Let me tell you a story (and, yes, I know you aren't a kid any more). Once upon a time, there was a man who wanted to change the world because there was so much poverty and inequality it hurt. He wrote a lot of stories about everything that was wrong, and hoped to make a difference. He was very hurt when people criticised his stories, so he said he wouldn't write any more as the world wasn't ready for him. Close to where he lived, another man dug a lot of earth closets (compost toilets to you and me; very wonderful things) and stopped hundreds of local people from getting ill and dying from a nasty disease called cholera. I've absolutely no idea if he ever hurt inside – the question never came up.

PS I think he was quite a dandy when he was young.

PPS Look around you: has everyone in your road already got an earth closet?

Dear Sloth

I'm renovating my house and putting the staircase in a new position. The old staircase (very seventies) had wide wooden rails that ran parallel to the stairs. It was dated but I liked the look and wanted the new staircase to be similar. I thought I'd make it look more contemporary by using one of those Deco-style tubular metal banisters you see in so many smart modern offices. I absolutely hate the idea of having to paint all those uprights on the more traditional type of staircase. Of course, I have to get permission to change my staircase around, and what do you think? They've changed the regulations and I'm not allowed to have parallel bars. Why? A child might use them as – guess what – a ladder! And they might fall over the edge and hurt their little selves. So I'm forced to have uprights, so close together the damn thing will look like a monkey cage – and I'll have to paint them. But perhaps not, because when I complained to the man from the Building Control Gestapo that I wouldn't be able to get my larger pieces of furniture up and down the stairs with this approved design, his reply was a classic. He suggested I left the rails off altogether until I moved out of the house. They could sign it off as finished at that stage. Apparently, that will be okay (though not, perhaps, any visiting kids). You couldn't make it up, could you?

Exasperated

Dear Exasperated

Exasperation is normal when you're trying to work on your house. Why do you humans want to 'improve' everything? It only causes problems. What was wrong with your other staircase, anyway? Didn't it go up to the next floor? If you'd left well alone, there wouldn't have been an issue, would there? If it weren't for the fact that this section is about the inadvisability of blaming others, I'd blame you. What is a building inspector but an expert? And if you will put yourself at the mercy of experts … Look around you: does any good ever come of them? I expect they'll soon be banning climbing equipment in school gyms as well. Take a tip from a sloth. The next time you feel the need to redesign your home, leave the top off. Not only will you be able to get the furniture in more easily, you'll have a nice, relaxing sun deck too. Ahhhhhh, lovely.

Dear Sloth

Don't you find it very distressing running a problem column like this? I'm one of nature's worriers, and I can't imagine how you cope. It would drive me to an early grave having to think about so many problems all day. I find it bad enough listening to the radio in the morning – so many terrible things happening in the world. And it's the same here in Britain. Everywhere I go I hear about people sick, people in trouble, awful children, rising crime, drought, hunger … Sometimes it seems as if this cannot possibly be a civilised country in the twenty-first century. It seems as though the advances of the last 50 years have all disappeared. I wonder what my father would think if he were alive. I'm sure he'd ask himself what he fought a war for; nobody seems in the least bit appreciative of the sacrifices that were made. It is all 'me, me, me' now, and everybody wants to have everything straightaway. There's no waiting or saving up or any of the old virtues. I can remember being told, 'I want, never gets', but the opposite seems to hold true today. Oh dear, this is all is a bit of a grumble, isn't it? But it does get me down, and there doesn't seem to be any escape. You always seem so serene and untroubled. However do you cope?

Distressed

Dear Distressed

The mention of sun decks in the last answer started me thinking about faraway warmth and the delights of the forest, so once I've shared some thoughts with you, I shall be ambling slowly off for a spell of well earned R and R. That, of course, is the true answer to your question, but it's not really what you want to know. What you really want to know is how you can learn to cope. And that's normal. In fact, everything you write is normal for human beings, judging by the postbag here anyway. You all seem to be in a permanent state of grumpy anxiety.

Now, a little light local moan is most enjoyable and beneficial, and to be thoroughly recommended to anyone who wants to stay sane, but we are not talking about that here; what we are talking about here, is a moaner's nuclear winter. There's nothing else but moan to be seen anywhere on the horizon, and the whole picture is cold, cold, cold; bleak, bleak, bleak. So cold and bleak that I'm going to break the habit of a lifetime and give you some direct advice. I think you are in need of a bit of help.

When a sloth feels a touch chilly, it stretches itself out on the top of the world and lets the sun shine straight down on it, warming itself all the way through to its belly. And do you know what else it does at the same time?

Nothing. Zero. Nothing at all. Zippo. Rien.

Can you imagine? It doesn't move a muscle, and not a single thought passes through its brain. It's bliss, I can promise you, but, ironically, it takes a bit of practice. To get such perfect mental clarity, you have to have an almost empty brain – natural enough for a sloth, I have to admit, but you humans may need to chuck some clutter out of yours. A bit like when you have to clear your loft of all those broken tennis rackets, empty boxes and unwanted presents before you move house. Clearing your brain will leave you feeling the way clearing your loft does – much, much cleaner and lighter.

Start by emptying your brain of all the worries you've colonised from other people. They're no use to you, and you can't do anything about them. You're simply hanging on to them because you're too possessive to let them go. But in truth they're none of your business. What's it to you if Mrs Brown's got high blood pressure or if there's a coup in a

Himalayan principality? What are you going to do about it? Or, for that matter, about things like EU budgets and the Dow Jones Index. Then, when you've chucked out all the worries that are other people's business, you can start on your own. This bit is really very easy. The principle is: if you can deal with it, do; if you can't, drop it. That's a sloth's logic anyway, and it seems to work.

Now all you need are a few tips on how to avoid collecting any more unwanted mental junk:

- For at least three days every week, switch off all news and current affairs programmes. That will give you time to get over one set of shocks completely before the next lot descend – and it won't make a scrap of difference to whether the world gets saved or not.

- Don't read newspapers. You'll find the world becomes a much nicer and less worrying place.

- Never drive during term time. In fact never drive more than you have to at any time.

- Avoid town centres on a Saturday. I'm sure I don't need to tell you why.

- Avoid friends with problems – but if you absolutely can't, practise switching off while saying, 'Oh, poor you!' at 30-second intervals.

- Never, ever read medical dictionaries (or look up symptoms on the internet).

All of that should empty your brain nicely. But just in case it won't stay that way, you may need to find nicer things to mull over while you're on your back in the sun. So you should start a little collection. Here's how:

- Make mental lists of what you love. We sloths like compost and green things, and gorgeous, gorgeous sleep – perhaps you do too.

- Do quiet things in quiet places. No gadgets, cars or gizmos. We like slowly swimming for miles and miles, but perhaps you prefer to wander about on dry land (someone has to). Potter about in the country with no particular aim or direction in mind. Pick out a nice blade of something green to chew and find yourself a gate to swing on. Smell the blossom, listen to the birds (I think you're safe from harpy eagles where you are). Lie on your back and watch the

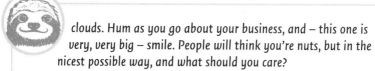

clouds. Hum as you go about your business, and – this one is very, very big – smile. People will think you're nuts, but in the nicest possible way, and what should you care?

- Collect warm, gentle, memories of doing nothing in particular.

- Be in the sun as much as you can. If you must, wear factor 950 for most of the time, but bare your skin for as long as it takes to get all the vitamin D you need. We all need plenty of sunshine in our lives.

- Now, this one pains me a bit, but we sloths are not pets and don't do houses, so you may have to learn to love some other types of creature too. You need some of the natural world in your home. Make a bit of space for a dog, a nice slow one that potters. Dogs are mostly just too empty-headed to have worries and so are good at taking things easy. (I can't possibly recommend cats – far too jet-propelled at times.) Dogs are also big on affection, which is much, much more relaxed than passion. (Cats have been known to take passion to extremes.)

I think you'll find that if you follow this advice – and do remember how precious it is – most of your worries will quietly melt away. There's no need to think the world has got any worse than it ever was. We sloths have been around for a while and can tell you it's pretty much the same. It's just taking up far more of your head space than is healthy.

- Slow down
- Tune it out
- Chill out

You'll soon wake up to a sunnier outlook.

And on that final, encouraging note, we'll leave the sloth, swinging gently where it fell asleep, high in the greenery, dappled with sunlight, and smiling softly to itself.

6

Slothful-filled

It's time to move on from the wit and wisdom of the proto-sloth to discover the sloth within. Deep joy can come with the rediscovery of our own, possibly shyer, more modest, home-grown variety. But first, let's remind ourselves of some of the reasons we called up the sloth from its extended slumbers in the first place.

It all started with the growing sensation many of us share that we are caught up in so much frenzied directionless activity today that it often feels as if we're going nowhere fast – that in fact we're on some kind of mad merry-go-round, and it is whirling us around so dizzyingly that it leaves us no chance to concentrate on anything other than the cries of the fairground hawkers, who are yelling out the attractions of growth, escalation and excess. Sure, we got onto it enthusiastically enough, but without realising how much we were leaving behind, and now it's too late to change our minds, so there's nothing for it but to hang on in there and enjoy its wondrous benefits. Choice, consumption, speed, growth, progress, perfectibility. No way down 24/7.

Of course, we're sure we should be having a whale of a time. It's just that we're so busy clinging on that we can't think about anything else, so have no way of checking. And we've absolutely no idea how we can get them to slow the blasted thing down.

Unless, of course, it gets stopped at Her Majesty's Pleasure (which, for the non-British among you, over here means a spell in prison). Then there'll be time and opportunity to realise that something other than speed and growth might have real significance. When the chips are down, we may discover that if we haven't provided ourselves with a well-stocked reservoir of memories, we don't have much we can truly call our own. Forget consumer rights acts, no one is entitled to buy good memories. Good memories, like good wine, have to be nurtured appreciatively and will always require a little bit of time and care in the laying down.

This is where the sloth came in. Because many of us now have little clue how to slow down for long enough to gather up memories in the first place, we have had to seek help in learning to take our lives more steadily. So we turned to the acme of arrested speed, the sultan of slow, the king of contemplativeness, to remind us that nature allows for large parts of some lives to be lived in a leisurely, sustainable, perfectly contented way, and that – at least at some time in the past, before we'd lost the art of living fully in the moment – our own lives were this way. We simply need to rediscover this natural, relaxed responsiveness to our own lives.

We've taken time to watch this delightfully laid-back creature and discover how it manages its own life so well. We've considered the idea that with a more leisurely response to life what we over-fried folks may be able to achieve is slow growth, SLOTH for short, rather than an outright closing down of everything – because no one is really interested in stopping the world and, anyway, mortgages still happen. And with many of us becoming increasingly disillusioned with the quality of our hectic lives, there is a real possibility that a slow-down can be made to work. It's not an unrealistic or unrealisable fantasy, and if enough of us, individually, are happy to take a little longer over the day to day business of living, we may just shift the balance. After all, it's hardly going to mean the collapse of society – quite the opposite, in fact.

With the loss of a natural harmonious relationship between ourselves and our lives, came our fixation on fixing everything, on living as though nothing could be more important than preparing to perfect the next part of our lives. We have believed for so long in the infallibility of action – any action – rather than no action that we've forgotten how to get pleasure simply from being. It's as though we've become frightened that we are just not enough, not quite good enough as ourselves, and that we have to hide behind an activity, a title, an intention or a substance to be worth anything much at all. We have to be a teacher, rather than a person in our own right who just happens to teach; we have to be a designer, rather than Sam, a nice bloke with a family and a lot of interests who spends part of his time designing. In order to *be* more, it seems we have to *do* more.

The sloth, on the other hand is much more involved in the *being* of its life than in the doing. If we listen to it carefully enough, it will tell us that only if we're frightened of who we are do we need to fill up every second of our time. If we want to prove to ourselves that we're not actually scared of simply *being alive*, then it's time we started to cut ourselves a bit of slack. When we are comfortable with taking pleasure in the present, we do not need to be constantly making plans for our next move.

DYNAMIC AS A DAISY

Some people have already made the radical decision that they are not going to be tyrannised by the 'need' to plan out their every move and fill out a time-flow chart for every second of their lives. They've been quietly (how else?) engaged with the process of rediscovering their inner sloth for a while. They've already realised that the key to pleasure is not to be found in constantly pushing the boundaries, of either speed or distance. For example they've discovered the benefits of giving up the nose-to-tail rush hour traffic and are either working from home or looking to relocate to smaller, slower, more neighbourly towns – towns where they might even risk letting their children walk or cycle to school! They are choosing self-organised local holidays over the dubious joys of ladling unthrilled kids on to long-haul flights flogging off to distant tourist destinations (and is there anywhere left that isn't just another tourist destination?) and finding that their children actually appreciate and enjoy this unpressured, unstructured approach much more.

And as neo-sloth Amanda Blinkhorn recognised, writing in *The Times* about the delights of the simple family holiday in the local countryside, it's time spent like this – in small, relaxed and not over-regulated ways – that brings with it the simple, precious, but today increasingly rare, sense of family togetherness:

> On the last night, sitting outside the tent ..., watching shooting stars with Nick, while the big ones read The Gruffalo to the little ones, we looked at each other and knew, you can keep your Barbados beach and your Tuscan villa – memories are made of this.

But it's not only precious pleasure that we get by doing the simpler slower things in life; there's also the opportunity to save large sums of money. It's a virtuous circle. If we don't need to spend so much to get the good times with our families, then the pressure to earn all the money that we used to need is lifted. So we can enjoy our less driven lives more.

THIS IS A LOCAL LIFE

The same principle works in other areas of life. For example, we can get similar benefits by sourcing our food more locally. There are savings in transportation costs, both financial and ecological; there's the inevitable boost to local quality and variety, and there's the ethical glow of gigantic proportions in the knowledge that we are not having our green beans watered and transported at the cost of other people's lives. If we bring food sourcing even more local, right up to our own back door, there are greater benefits still – better health from all that digging and eating all those fruits and vegetables, massive savings in money, big improvements in flavour and quality, and the sense of warmth and achievement that comes with working together as a family to produce something that we can then enjoy cooking and eating together.

RELISH THAT INNER TIME

There are other home-grown things we can enjoy, too, like hobbies and play. We don't need to spend fortunes on electronic equipment, or on busily 'enjoying' what the leisure 'industry' (and there's an interesting word) dictates we should do with our precious leisure time. We can be free to be, well, free of all that. A study of 134 Nobel prize winners found that two-thirds of them said there was a connection between their imaginary world and their discoveries, which suggests that simple contemplative time offers huge creative advantages. It has also been suggested that children who call their activities play, rather than work, grow up to be more academically successful, so we can in good conscience let our kids off the hook of having to work so hard at their play as well. Let's take away their mobile phones and their computers for a bit and (having fed them on decent food, not hyper-active-making junk) let them be nerdy, local, home-grown kids, climbing the odd tree (and perhaps gazing down from the canopy), riding their bikes, skimming stones over water, lying on their backs in the sun, exploring what's around them, and perhaps even fighting their own fights from time to time and picking themselves up when they fall down.

Many older people have also been enjoying the discovery that what were once considered nerdy hobbies are now cool. Stamp collecting is booming, so is bird watching; the knitting section is the must-visit department at London department store John Lewis; old-fashioned board games are selling fast; Hornby model train sales were worth £17 million in 2004; and tapestries are nearly as popular as they were in the Middle Ages. More and more of us are discovering how totally satisfying and relaxing it can be simply to allow ourselves the freedom to become utterly absorbed in an unhurried interest or in a soothing, repetitive rhythmic movement. It's the deep pleasure of living fully in the moment. It's the warm glow of satisfaction that comes with doing something slow and concentrated. Especially if we do it in the company of people who are just as absorbed and in no more of a hurry to move on than we are.

Rich in time

Taking time – putting ourselves back in charge of it, taking time out, taking our time, taking time over. Time in the country, time by the sea, time on our own, time on our backs, time for tea, time for someone. Making time for ourselves. In our own time.

We don't need to be at the mercy of time, especially if, from time to time, we allow ourselves to ditch those tyrannical sidekicks of time, our watches, mobiles, computers, radio stations and energetic strategies for holding back time (which you must admit is a pretty damn strenuous idea in the first place).

After all, the notion that time is something that is about to swamp us whenever we take our eyes off the clock for a couple of seconds is not a pleasant one, and having to feel some kind of moral and physical duty to hold it back is just stressful and overwhelming. We'd all be much better off accepting the inevitability of time, bobbing along on its surface and calling ourselves rich in the possession of it.

In a recent book, *The Joy of Laziness*, two German doctors, Peter Axt and his daughter Michaela, go so far as to suggest that trying to hold back time by excessive exercising, the route so many of us take in our result-driven society, may actually result in the opposite effect, premature ageing. They say that the stress and anxiety hormone, cortisol, which is a by-product of high levels of exercise, can raise the levels of free radicals in our bodies and so lower both our immune system and what they call our life energy. Rather than expend our energies on a losing battle, we'd do better to enjoy the time we have, eat a healthy diet, and, wait for it, enjoy plenty of laughter.

Brilliant. We can save the time, save the money (and therefore the need to earn it) and save our health simultaneously. What a turn up for the books. All we need to do is focus on enjoying things more – and that we can learn from our own children, who have easy laughter down to a fine art. Babies and very young children smile and laugh simply out of their delight in being alive in their own, very clever, bodies. We only have to see them intensely focused on grabbing hold of something for the first time, or taking their first wobbly step, or watching a shadow moving on a wall, to know how wonderful life is to them. Their concentration and their pleasure in what they are seeing or doing are simply entrancing to watch. They have the same unhurried relationship with time as our other favourite model, the sloth. Each tiny move, each little adjustment and achievement is an enormous source of satisfaction for them.

By rediscovering both the baby and the sloth within us we start to appreciate in the purest possible way that simply being alive is enough in itself, thank you very much, and that, although we quite like other goodies too, they'll never be able to give us anything like the pleasure that we can get, if we want, from simply being us.

Enjoying being wonderful us can be greatly enhanced if we're prepared to pull the plug on some of the other, duller things we've been doing, such as watching mind-numbing TV shows; driving here, there and everywhere to buy things we don't need; drinking ourselves stupid; working ourselves into a state of anxiety about things we can do nothing about; and just generally trying too hard to be something we are not. We're able to concentrate so much more of our energy on enjoying being what we genuinely are, amazing miracles of natural engineering that are capable of experiencing deep pleasure, when we let ourselves do just that.

So let's turn off our TV sets and enjoy the full sensory pleasure of the good food that we've grown. Let's listen to the birdsong without the intervening sound of radios, mobile phones, whirring computers or traffic. Let's experience the texture of surfaces and feel our fingers without also needing to be doing something with them. Let's close our eyes and smell the flowers. Let's lie in a bath and listen to Mozart – and not feel we should be busy doing anything else at all.

THE END PRODUCT

As we know, sloths are very big on end products, so what is the end product of our tutorial with the sloth?

As we know by now, there's no *should* involved, but hopefully the end product is the freedom to say that rushing after every opportunity to 'perfect' ourselves just isn't on any more. That there's no need to get stressed every time we find ourselves in a queue because, quite frankly, we're not going anywhere that special. That there's more to living than doing, doing, doing every minute. That someone has to stop the frenzy (which isn't that much fun anyway) and it might as well be me. That we are not all going to have it all, and if we did, who'd want it? That there's more fun to be had in a minute with a dog in a field than in all the Game Boys in the world. That we like local, we like fresh, we like home, we like family.

And having given ourselves permission to dump the pressure, it's loving the sense of relaxation – even in a traffic jam – that comes from living in the moment and enjoying what's there to be enjoyed, whether that's taking the opportunity to listen to the music we like, or appreciating the flowers at the roadside, or admiring the way our hands are so clever on the steering wheel.

It's a relaxed, shaggy shape, hanging dreamily from a branch, with its head tucked in, a smile on its face. And nearby is another one the same, and then another and another. And as we track back and look upwards, we see there's an undiscovered world full of them, stretching away for miles and miles, reaching out as far as our very own back garden, where there's a (perhaps shaggy) shape, relaxing, swinging dreamily in a hammock, chin tucked in, hat pulled down, a soft, self-contented smile spreading over our face.

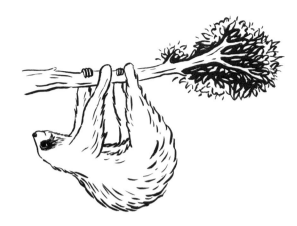

Index

Page references in *italics* indicate case studies

Index

Index